1

Introduction

Anyone can write a long program; what is really difficult is to write an interesting program in only one line. That is why I make no apologies for opening this book with what may well be the shortest games program on record. Oh, it really works – and it's interesting, too, for it times your reactions to the nearest one-hundredth of a second. Try it at any time, especially when you've had a few drinks! When prompted, tap any key as fast as you can.

Here is the entire listing:

```
F.X = 1TORND(1000):N.:P."GO!":TI. = 0:X$ = GE.:P.TI./100;"
secs."
```

One is able to write like that because Acorn have provided the BBC Microcomputer with two interesting and useful features that affect us both – myself as the writer and you as the reader of this book. The first is that any number of statements may be placed in one multi-command line, extending to no less than six print lines on the screen, with automatic wrap-around taking place at the end of the line. This means that in many published listings there are some fairly heavy-looking blocks of text to be copied into your computer. I have tried to avoid that, but here and there this avoidance in fact *lengthens* the listing because particular logic structures cannot be used. Therefore, although expert readers will be able to shorten the listings a little, neophytes will find them easier to read and understand.

The second point is that the BBC computer allows shortened forms of commands, like 'P.' for 'PRINT', 'E.' for 'ENDPROC', and so on. It is well worth your while knowing these, for they can cut your typing time enormously. They are listed in the *User Guide*.

If you wish to check the single-line program above, the following is the extended form; at least it allows you to follow more easily

2 IntroductionIntroduction

what the program does. Line 10 ensures a random start, eliminating anticipation.

```
10 FOR X = 1 TO RND(1000):NEXT
20 PRINT"GO!!"
30 TIME = 0
40 X$ = GET$
50 PRINT "You took ";TIME/100;" seconds"
```

Of course, the game is not perfect, and we ought to include an *FX15,1 command at the end of line 30, but at least it illustrates the point: that writers have to steer a narrow course between on the one hand making listings so dense that they become impossible to understand – and easy to lose your way in – and on the other hand making them so spread out that the book is soon filled and the reader does not get full value for money.

There is another point of particular interest to owners of OS versions 1.0 and up: the use of the colour graphics commands in Mode 7. By holding down the SHIFT key and pressing the Function Keys f1 to f9, various print colours are obtained. Unfortunately this cannot be shown in printed form, as the single byte thus stored in the program creates havoc when received by printers – usually a graphics symbol is printed, but anything goes. For this reason, these commands are shown in full as PRINT CHR$(129), etc. Readers may make a considerable saving in typing time and effort by substituting:

CHR$129	SHIFT−f1	(Red text)
CHR$130	SHIFT−f2	(Green text)
CHR$131	SHIFT−f3	(Yellow text)
CHR$132	SHIFT−f4	(Blue text)
CHR$133	SHIFT−f5	(Magenta text)
CHR$134	SHIFT−f6	(Cyan text)
CHR$135	SHIFT−f7	(White text)
CHR$136	SHIFT−f8	(Flashing text)
CHR$137	SHIFT−f9	(Steady text)

Another very welcome feature of the BBC machine is that it supports procedures. This not only encourages good programming practice, but enables sections of program to be tested and proved in isolation. As an example of this, on page 4 are listed a number of interesting and useful procedures that are used many times in this book. It is recommended that the reader types and saves them once only – on disk or tape – and reloads them when starting to copy a new program. The method is:

(a) Copy the procedures exactly as printed
(b) Type *SPOOL PROCS (Return)
(c) If using tape, start recording
(d) Type LIST (Return)
(e) When list is finished, type *SPOOL (Return).

BBC Micro Programs in BASIC

Derrick Daines

Newnes Technical Books

Newnes Technical Books
is an imprint of the Butterworth Group
which has principal offices in
London, Boston, Durban, Singapore, Sydney, Toronto, Wellington

First published in 1984

© **Butterworth & Co (Publishers) Ltd, 1984**
   Borough Green, Sevenoaks, Kent TN15 8PH, England

British Library Cataloguing in Publication Data

Daines, Derrick
   BBC Micro programs in BASIC
   1. Electronic games   2. BBC Microcomputer
   —Programming   3. Basic (Computer program language)
   I. Title
   794.8'028'5424   GV1469.2

   ISBN 0-408-01415-6

Library of Congress Cataloging in Publication Data

Daines, Derrick
   BBC Micro programs in BASIC
   1. BBC Microcomputer—Programming.   2. Basic
   (Computer program language)   I. Title   II. Title:
   B.B.C. Micro programs in B.A.S.I.C.
   QA76.8.B35D35 1984   001.64'.2   83-23712

   ISBN 0-408-01415-6

Photoset by Butterworths Litho Preparation Department
Printed in England by Whitstable Litho Ltd, Whitstable, Kent

Contents

The publishers gratefully acknowledge the assistance of Pace Software Supplies Ltd, X-Data Ltd and Cumana Ltd in the preparation of this book.

The procedures are then stored on tape or disk in ASCII format (not BASIC). When starting the copy of a new listing from this book, rewind the tape and type:

   *EXEC PROCS (Return)

Start the tape and the procedures will be loaded in. If desired, the procedures could be SAVEd and LOADed as a BASIC program, but the advantage of doing it in the way outlined is that they can be added to an existing program at any time, without destroying what is already in memory.

PROCTITLE
The procedure prints a title in double height, with a decorative design above and below. The design is in blue, with the title yellow. The only parameter that needs passing to it is the title X$, with the procedure automatically placing it in the centre. Please note that the procedure works properly in Mode 7 only; indeed, the calling program might include a MODE 7 command, which would clear the screen and prepare for the title.

PROCDBL
This procedure is in the *User Guide* and I have altered it slightly so that the position on the screen is determinable – the X% and Y% values passed – as is the colour, in C%· The text to be printed in double height is passed in X$·

PROCBOX
A longish procedure, but enormously useful. It will print a box of any size, in any colour, in any position on the screen, outlining it with a strong line. In addition, it will if desired print a number of white dots within the box to indicate the maximum number of input characters allowable, and accept input, overprinting the dots. Deletion is allowed up to the time when RETURN is pressed, while if the user attempts to enter more characters than the program allows, the ultimate character is altered. In other words, the user cannot overflow the box.
   Mode 7 graphics are used. The parameters passed are:

X%   Horizontal tab position of left edge
Y%   Vertical tab of bottom edge minus 1
L%   The length: the number of character spaces allowed inside
H%   The height: the number of lines allowed inside
C%   Colour: from 145 to 151 for white to red
F%   Flag, where 0 = input desired, 1 = no input
On exit, X$ holds the input line, if any, and this will be tested by the calling routine.

```
10000 DEFPROCTITLE(X$)
10010 PRINTCHR$132;STRING$(19,"Oo")
10020 PROCDBL((36-LEN(X$))/2,3,131,X$)
10030 PRINT'CHR$132;STRING$(19,"Oo")
10040 ENDPROC
10050
10060 DEFPROCDBL(X%,Y%,C%,X$)
10070 PRINTTAB(X%,Y%);CHR$141;CHR$C%;X$
10080 PRINTTAB(X%,Y%+1);CHR$141;CHR$C%;X$
10090 ENDPROC
10100
10110 DEFPROCBOX(X%,Y%,L%,H%,C%,F%)
10120 LOCALV%,W%,I%,J%:REM - MODE7 ONLY
10130 PRINTTAB(X%,Y%);
10140 V%=VPOS:W%=POS:PRINTTAB(W%,V%-H%);CHR$C%;"7";
10150 FORI%=0TOL%+1:PRINT"£";:NEXT:PRINT"k"
10160 PRINTTAB(W%,V%+1);CHR$C%;"u";
10170 FORI%=0TOL%+1:PRINT"p";:NEXT:PRINT"z"
10180 FORJ%=V%-H%+1TOV%:PRINTTAB(W%,J%);CHR$C%;"5":NEXT
10190 FORJ%=V%-H%+1TOV%
10200 PRINTTAB(W%+L%+3,J%);CHR$C%;"j":NEXT
10210 IF F%GOTO10320
10220 PRINTTAB(W%+2,V%);CHR$135;
10230 FORI%=1TOL%:PRINT".";:NEXT
10240 PRINTTAB(W%+3,V%);:X$=""
10250 G$=GET$:IF ASCG$=13 GOTO10320
10260 IF LENX$=L%OR ASCG$=127 GOTO10280
10270 PRINT G$;:X$=X$+G$:GOTO10250
10280 IF X$="" GOTO10250
10290 X$=LEFT$(X$,LENX$-1):PRINTCHR$8;
10300 IF ASCG$<>127 GOTO10270
10310 PRINT".";CHR$8;:GOTO10250
10320 ENDPROC
10330
10340 DEFPROCRET
10350 PRINTTAB(5,19);CHR$131;"Press";
10360 PRINTCHR$132;CHR$157:CHR$129;"RETURN ";CHR$156:
10370 G$=GET$:CLS:ENDPROC
10380
10390 DEFPROCWARBLE
10400 FORS%=1TO20:SOUND1,-12,30,1
10410 SOUND1,-12,100,1:NEXT:ENDPROC
10420
10430 DEFPROCBOING
10440 SOUND 0,-15,80,2:FOR S%=-15 TO 0
10450 SOUND1,S%,20+S%,2:NEXT:ENDPROC
```

PROCRET

The instruction to the user, 'Press RETURN', is so often used that it is well worth while having a little procedure to give it and to wait until a key is pressed. This procedure prints a very attractive and eye-catching instruction, with 'Press' in yellow, and 'RETURN' in red on a dark blue background. No parameters are passed to the procedure, but the TAB position may require alteration to suit different circumstances.

PROCWARBLE
A little sound routine used as an audible signal that the user has won a game or done something good.

PROCBOING
Another little sound for the opposite effect. It sounds rather like a recalcitrant sofa spring and nobody can doubt its message!

Close examination of the above procedures in various parts of the book will reveal small but significant differences here and there. This is because I have taken the view that readers interested in only one or two programs will not wish to duplicate these procedures as outlined above and so will not need some of their features; PROCBOX is a case in point. In the individual listings, therefore, I have included only those features needed by that particular program. If you copy the listings as shown you may be confident that they will run correctly. On the other hand, if you follow the method outlined above, re-using the saved procedures, the programs will still run correctly, although features will be included in a particular program that may not be used within it.

A good illustration of this is PROCBOX, which in its complete form allows the user to type an input within the box, the length of input being indicated by a number of white dots. Many of the listed programs do not require this facility, which (together with the necessary ability to delete or correct an input before RETURN) makes PROCBOX rather long. The listings not requiring an input of this nature therefore do not show this part of PROCBOX.

In the pursuit of readability, I have spread out the listings a little by the insertion of empty lines. These show a line number only. Empty lines may cause a little bewilderment to newcomers, because of course if you type a line number only, followed by RETURN, nothing is recorded. Moreover, if there was a line with that number, it is now erased! In fact, the empty lines are easy to achieve: if you wish to incorporate them into your own programs for the purpose of breaking up the listings and making them easier to read, the trick is to type the line number and then one or more spaces, before pressing RETURN.

One other trick to aid readability – which unfortunately we cannot show in printed form – is to incorporate colour into REM statements. If you do this, note that the colour byte mentioned earlier MUST be preceded by inverted commas:

250 REM " This remark is in colour

where the CHR$131 byte (or whatever) follows the inverted com-
mas. It is also worth noting that, if a line is never processed during
run time, the REM is not needed, so that

250 " This remark can be in colour
260 " and so can this, as long as they are not processed.

are perfectly OK and will always show in colour when the program
is listed. Such lines are very usefully placed before procedures in
long programs and allow you to scan a listing swiftly. For obvious
reasons, these tricks have not been incorporated in the current
listings.

Tired of all that typing? All of the programs listed in this book are
available on cassette from:

Leasalink Viewdata Ltd
Electron House
Bridge Street
Sandiacre
Nottingham NG10 5BA

Leasalink are also main distributors for the BBC computer.

2

Quickdraw and 100 metres sprint

'Quickdraw' takes the idea of the timed response one stage further. We suppose a Western situation, with the user required to type the word BANG as quickly as possible. The computer will keep track of the best time.

In line 10 we set the best time impossibly high, because otherwise no-one would ever better it. We ask for the user's name and then in line 40 have him or her wait for an indeterminate time before challenging him to draw and fire on line 50. You should be able to follow the listing quite easily, except perhaps for line 60, where *FX15,0 is a command to flush the internal buffers. This prevents the user cheating by having the word BANG already typed in before the 'Draw!' prompt appears. This would be possible because anything typed is stored in a buffer and not until RETURN is pressed does the BBC computer start to operate on it. Flushing the buffers means that the user is allowed to start typing only after the prompt appears.

Variables

BEST	The best (i.e. shortest) time so far recorded
NAME$	Name of current user
X	General counter
TIME	The internal elapsed-time counter
X$	Required input from the user
T	Time in seconds taken by the current user
BEST$	Name of the player with BEST time

100 metres sprint

Quickdraw will sustain user interest for only a little while, but at least one best-selling program extended the idea to a Computer

```
10 BEST=999
20 INPUT "Please type your name",NAME$
30 PRINTTAB(3,12);"Ready"
40 FOR X=1 TO RND(1000):NEXT
50 PRINTTAB(RND(30),RND(15));"Draw!"
60 TIME=0:*FX15,0
70 REPEAT
80 INPUT X$
90 UNTIL X$="BANG"
95 T=TIME/100
100 PRINT;"You drew and fired in ";T;" seconds"
110 IF T>=BEST GOTO 145
115 PRINT "The best so far!"
120 BEST=T
130 BEST$=NAME$
135 PROCRET:CLS
140 GOTO 20
145 PRINT "You're dead!"'
150 PRINT "The best shot so far is ";BEST$;","
160 PRINT "who took only ";BEST;" seconds"'
165 PROCRET:CLS
170 GOTO 20
```

Decathlon, with ten different keyboard responses for the ten different events. If you like button-bashing programs, there's an idea for you! Merely in the spirit of showing you how one would go about it, here is a listing that would simulate the 100 metres sprint. You are required to type L and R alternately 100 times.

The listing is very similar to the last. The only additional information you need in order to understand it is that the GET$ command does not require the RETURN key to be pressed, so playing is quite literally L and R alternately.

```
10 BEST=999
40 PRINT "On your marks";
50 FOR X=1 TO RND(5000):NEXT
70 PRINT "GO!":*FX15,0
80 TIME=0
90 FOR X=1 TO 100
100 REPEAT
110 G$=GET$
120 UNTIL G$="L"
130 REPEAT
140 G$=GET$
150 UNTIL G$="R"
160 NEXT X
170 PRINT "Your time was ";TIME/100;" seconds"
```

3

Market day

The *User Guide* specifies that there are 16 colours available on the BBC Micro. This is rather misleading, since eight of these are flashing versions of the others. On the other hand, the Guide says nothing about innumerable other effects easily obtained, such as striped colours in infinite variety. As soon as I saw this effect, there immediately shot into my mind the thought of deckchair material, or the gay striped canvas that one often sees over market stalls. So this little program was born.

The program does nothing but print a number of squares in striped and plain colours, the squares growing larger towards the

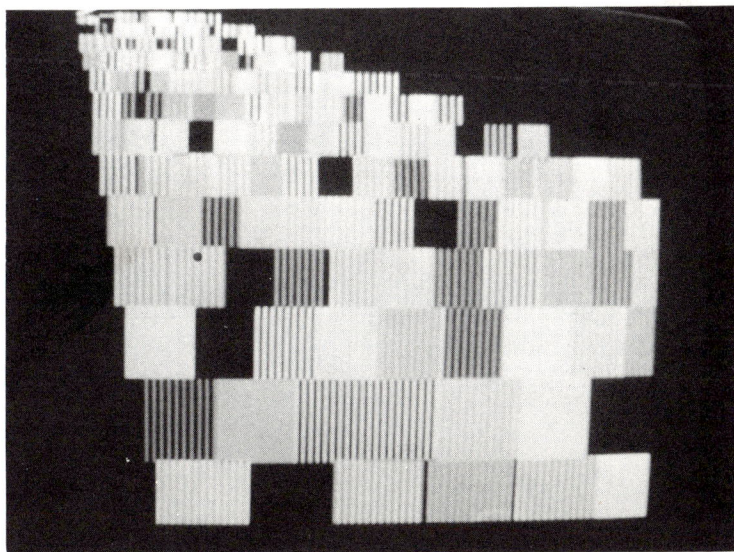

bottom of the screen and thus giving an illusion of depth. The various stripes and colours are randomly chosen, so each run gives a different set. If nothing else, it illustrates the wide variety of effects that are obtainable on the BBC computer.

Lines 30, 40 and 50 change colours 8–15 (the flashing varieties) into steady versions, but the single command *FX10,0 would do exactly the same thing. The next few lines fix the width and height of the squares in each row, with the colour – striped or plain – chosen in line 120. Line 180 stops the program when the bottom of the screen is reached.

Variables

X	General counter
ROW	The height up the screen of the top of each square
SIZE	The width of each square
COLUMN	The position from the left edge of the screen

```
 10 REM - Market Day
 20 MODE2
 30 FOR X=0 TO 7
 40 VDU19,X+8,X,0,0,0
 50 NEXT
 60 ROW=1100
 70 REPEAT
 80 SIZE=(60-ROW/20)*4
 90 ROW=ROW-SIZE-2
100 FOR COLUMN=1 TO 15
110 MOVE COLUMN*SIZE,ROW-100
120 GCOLRND(255),0
130 PLOT0,SIZE,0
140 PLOT81,-SIZE,SIZE
150 PLOT1,SIZE,-SIZE
160 PLOT81,0,SIZE
170 NEXT
180 UNTIL ROW<=0
```

4

Pattern maker

There is not a lot that one can say about this program. There are many similar pattern-drawing programs published and available, but just when one thinks that one has got this one sorted out and can predict more or less what it is going to do next, it goes and does something different. Part of the interest is that, like the previous program, much play is made of switching colours. As a consequence, the program may redraw the entire display in black (invisibly) before abruptly revealing it. Occasionally at the beginning it may switch itself to black for some time, so don't be afraid of pressing the ESCAPE key and then restarting it. Another point is that the program needs to run for at least ten minutes, especially in order to

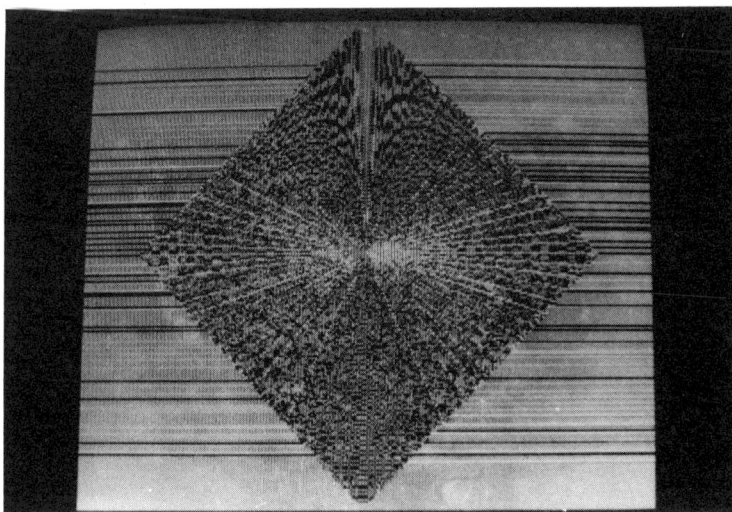

allow background colours to develop, when of course the all-black display is very much a rarity.

If you try changing line 20 to Mode 2, more colours are available on the screen at once, but the definition is chunkier. In addition, some moiré patterns are not discernible. Actually, you can play around with quite a few lines, especially 50, 80, 90, 100 and 240, changing the numeric values in these lines. You can also try the effect of removing the duplicated line at 130. Have fun!

```
 10 REM Pattern Maker
 20 MODE1
 30 VDU29,640;512;
 40 REPEAT
 50 GCOLRND(5)-1,RND(8)-1
 60 X%=510
 70 Y%=0
 80 I%=RND(30)+4
 90 P%=(RND(11)-1)*8+3+RND(4)
100 L%=RND(500)
110 REPEAT
120 MOVE0,0
130 MOVE0,0
140 PLOTP%,X%,Y%
150 MOVE0,0
160 PLOTP%,X%,-Y%
170 MOVE0,0
180 PLOTP%,-X%,-Y%
190 MOVE0,0
200 PLOTP%,-X%,Y%
210 X%=X%-I%
220 Y%=Y%+I%
230 UNTIL X%<L%
240 VDU19,RND(8)-1,RND(8)-1,0,0,0
250 UNTIL0
```

5

Time bomb

The story behind the game is well explained in lines 580 to 720 of the listing, so we may proceed to a discussion of the program. There are seven digits to be found and these are placed in the array N%(X). The box of explosives is drawn using Mode 7 graphics, which explains that weird and wonderful PRINT statement of line 122. CHR$149 is the command to print graphics magenta, so the strange mixture of characters is translated into block graphics, representing the sticks of dynamite poking up out of the box. Similarly, on line 90, X$ and E$ are constructed of commands to start and stop background printing in red, thus allowing us to draw the box and its windows with ease. See the Introduction for an easier way of doing this.

The user's input is accepted on line 250, without use of the RETURN key, which speeds things up. The input is compared with the current secret digit in lines 260 to 290, with the appropriate high or low tones being sounded. In practice the player will not want to keep looking at the timer counting down, because this will slow him. Instead, he will find that listening to the tones is quite sufficient. When a digit has been found it is displayed in the bomb window and the program moves automatically and swiftly to the next digit. Although very little time is allowed for winning, and although the user may not win for some time, nevertheless it can be beaten by anyone with a little nerve and concentration. Considering the times that we live in, I have thought it advisable to keep the tone of the game light and humorous.

PROCUPDATE is responsible for the timer countdown, while PROCCRASH gives the explosive sound and PROCWARBLE a happy warbling sound when the bomb has successfully been defused.

Variables

Q$	User input string
N%(0) to N%(6)	The seven secret digits
X%	General counter
Z%	Starting allowance in seconds
X$	Graphics line start
E$	Graphics line end
G%	Player's input digit
T%	Time left in seconds
C%	Colour of double-height print

```
 10 REM - Time bomb
 20 CLS:PROCDBL(5,5,129,"TIME-BOMB")
 30 INPUT''"Do you want instructions",Q$
 40 IF Q$="Y" PROCINSTR
 50 DIM N%(6),S%(6):VDU23;8202;0;0;0
 60
 70 REM - Set-up
 80 FOR X%=0 TO 6:N%(X%)=RND(10)-1:S%(X%)=0:NEXT
 90 Z%=RND(10)+10:X$=CHR$129+CHR$157+CHR$135:E$=CHR$156
100
110 REM - Draw box of dynamite
120 CLS:PRINTTAB(5,3);:RESTORE:FOR X%=1 TO 23:READ Y%
122 PRINTCHR$(Y%);:NEXT
125 DATA149,248,248,53,232,244,245,126,52,124,126,234
126 DATA32,244,224,52,53,248,232,53,244,234,52
130 PRINTTAB(3,4);X$;TAB(50);E$
140 PRINTTAB(3,5);X$;" E X P L O S I V E S   "
150 PRINTTAB(0,6);X$;TAB(33);E$
160 PRINTTAB(3,7);X$;TAB(27);E$
180 PROCUPDATE
190 PRINTTAB(3)X$;"     ":E$;STRING$(15," ");X$;"    ";E$
200 PRINTTAB(3);X$;TAB(30);E$
210 TIME=0:X%=0
220
230 REM - Game loop
240
250 REPEAT:G%=INKEY(0)-48
260 IF G%<0GOTO300
270 IF G%=N%(X%) VDU7:S%(X%)=G%:X%=X%+1:IF X%=7 GOTO400
280 IF G%<N%(X%) SOUND 1,-15,50,1
290 IF G%>N%(X%) SOUND 1,-15,500,1
300 T%=Z%-TIME/100:PROCUPDATE
310 UNTIL TIME>=Z%*100
320
330 REM - Big bang
340 CLS:PROCCRASH:*FX15,1
350 PROCDBL(5,3,129,"OH DEAR!")
360 PRINT''"That's another fine pair of eyebrows"
370 PRINT"you've lost, Stanley!":GOTO430
```

```
380
390 REM - Win
400 PROCDBL(2,16,130,"C O N G R A T U L A T I O N S !")
410 PROCWARBLE:PRINT'"YOU DID IT AND SAVED THE OLD SCHOOL!"
420 PRINT"The Head kisses you on both cheeks!"
430 *FX15,0
435 INPUT'"PLAY AGAIN (Y-N)",Q$:IF Q$="Y" GOTO80 ELSE END
440
450 DEFPROCDBL(X%,Y%,C%,X$)
460 PRINTTAB(X%,Y%)CHR$141;CHR$C%;X$
470 PRINTTAB(X%,Y%+1)CHR$141;CHR$C%;X$:ENDPROC
480
490 DEFPROCUPDATE
500 PRINTTAB(3,8)X$;"    TIME:";T%;X$;;TAB(27);E$
510 PRINTTAB(3)X$;TAB(30);E$
520 PRINTTAB(3)X$;"   ";E$;STRING$(15," "):X$;"   ";E$
530 PRINTTAB(3):X$;"   ";E$;"   ";
540 FOR Q%=0TO6:PRINT;S%(Q%);"   ";:NEXT:PRINT:X$;"   ";E$
550 ENDPROC
560
570 DEFPROCINSTR
580 CLS:PRINT''"The dastardly Sir Simon Ffoul-Enuff has"
590 PRINT"planted a bomb in the refreshment tent"
600 PRINT"at your school fete! It is bolted to"
610 PRINT"the tea urn and so cannot be moved. The"
620 PRINT"only way for you to save civilisation"
630 PRINT"as we know it, is to render"
640 PRINT"the bomb harmless."'
650 PRINT"There are seven numbers to find. If"
660 PRINT"your guess is low, the mechanism gives"
670 PRINT"a low note, while if it is high, then"
680 PRINT"a high note is emitted."
690 PRINT'"A beep tells you that you have found"
700 PRINT"that number & can move on to the next."
710 PRINT'"You have only a few seconds."''
720 PRINT"Good luck!":INPUT'" Press RETURN...",Q$
730 ENDPROC
740
750 DEFPROCWARBLE
760 FORS%=1TO20:SOUND1,-12,30,1
770 SOUND1,-12,100,1:NEXT:ENDPROC
780
790 DEFPROCCRASH
800 FOR Q%=-160TO0:SOUND0,Q%/10,6,1:NEXT:ENDPROC
```

6

Bicycle wheel

One of the most useful facilities on the BBC Micro is the ability to change any logical colour at will, with the VDU19 command. By switching chosen colours from black to, say, yellow and back again, we can give the illusion of rapid motion, which is precisely what this program does.

We choose Mode 1 for the higher definition that it gives us. This mode allows four colours on the screen at once, but we will be using only two while the bicycle wheel is spinning; these will be black and yellow. Remember, however, that although only four are allowed, we still have a genuine eight to play with.

The *FX9,0 command has the same effect as *FX10 mentioned previously; that of making the flashing colours steady. Line 40 places the origin of the graphics in the centre of the screen and then we call PROCPOLY 15 times. PROCPOLY draws a large central hexagon and is well worth saving for other purposes. The hexagon is outlined and then each point is connected to every other point. Each hexagon is drawn in a different colour, although (again) it is worth noticing that because Mode 1 allows only four, the appearance at this stage is of overlapping hexagons in red, yellow and white. Internally, however, BBC BASIC considers them as all different.

When the hexagons are drawn, the REPEAT–UNTIL loop of lines 80–140 is entered, with UNTIL 0 signifying 'for ever'. At each pass through the loop we have another FOR–NEXT loop inside it, which switches the sequence colour on at line 100 and off at line 120. Line 110 provides a tiny delay of three one-hundredths of a second. The effect of all this is a most convincing impression of a bicycle wheel revolving rather smartly. Try altering the bracketed value of line 110 for a faster or slower effect, but if you speed it up too much, the image does not have time to form completely before it is

wiped out, and so it becomes less satisfactory and may even
disappear altogether.

Variables

X(0) to X(5)	X,Y co-ordinates of each of the 6 points
Y(0) to Y(5)	of the hexagon currently being drawn
X	General counter
K	A dummy
R	The radius of the polygon
C	Colour of polygon
BIAS	Angle of twist (in radians)
A	Angle in radians
PI	BASIC standard variable for pi (surprise!)
L	Counter for the chords connecting points

```
 10 REM Bicycle Wheel
 20 DIM X(5),Y(5)
 30 MODE1:*FX9,0
 40 VDU29,600;500;
 50 FOR X=1 TO 15
 60 PROCPOLY(500,X,X*15)
 70 NEXT
 80 REPEAT
 90 FOR X=1 TO 3
100 VDU19,X,3,0,0,0
110 K=INKEY(3)
120 VDU19,X,0,0,0,0
130 NEXT
140 UNTIL 0
150
160 DEFPROCPOLY(R,C,BIAS)
170 GCOL0,C
180 FOR SIDE=0 TO 5
190 A=SIDE*2*PI/5+BIAS
195 X(SIDE)=R*COSA:Y(SIDE)=R*SINA
200 NEXT SIDE
210 FOR SIDE=1 TO 5
220 FOR L=SIDE TO 5
222 MOVE X(SIDE),Y(SIDE):DRAW X(L),Y(L)
224 NEXT L
230 NEXT SIDE
240 ENDPROC
```

7

Plates

In this program, a slightly different version of PROCPOLY fills in the polygon in a chosen colour before joining each point to every other point. As before, the radius of the polygon is the variable R, but the program calling the procedure gradually reduces R in line 120, thus smaller and smaller polygons are superimposed upon each other.

The number of sides is variable from 1 to 30 and of course the colours are randomly chosen for each polygon. A point of particular interest is the GCOL command of line 230:

GCOLRND(5)−1,RND(4)−1

A perusal of this command in the *User Guide* will show that the result is that the chords drawn in line 260 can be simply drawn, ANDed, ORed or inverted. The effect can be extremely difficult to describe, but is caused by a line being drawn and then another drawn crossing it. In many circumstances, where the two lines cross, both lines are wiped out. Since a multiple-sided polygon will have many such lines crossing each other, the effect can be quite extraordinary, rather like the tightly crinkled petals of a carnation, and quite beautiful in close-up, although some of this effect is lost if you are using the domestic television instead of a colour monitor.

Overall, then, the program simply draws superimposed polygons with or without criss-crossing lines, the polygons getting smaller and smaller, so the total effect is exactly like an expensive dinner plate with an intricate design. As is usual with computer-generated graphics, some colour combinations are quite stunning.

Variables

X(0) to X(30)	The X,Y co-ordinates of the points of
Y(0) to Y(30)	the current polygon
R	Polygon radius
S	Number of sides
C	Colour to be blocked in
A	Angle to be turned
L	Count of chords

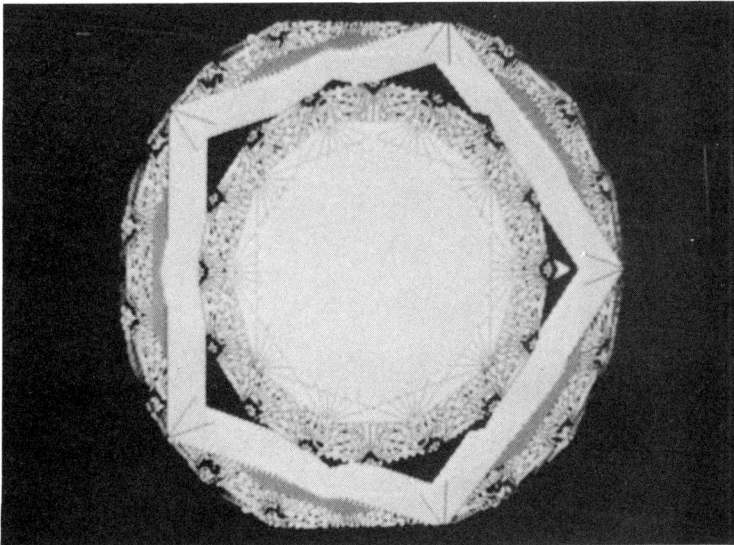

```
10 REM - Plates
20 DIM X(30),Y(30)
30 MODE1
40 VDU29,650;512;
50 REPEAT
60 R=550
70 S=RND(18)+2
80 MOVE R,0
90 MOVE 10,10
100 C=RND(4)
110 PROCPOLY(R,S,C)
120 R=R-RND(100)
130 IF R>50 GOTO 70
140 UNTIL 0
150
160 DEFPROCPOLY(R,S,C)
170 GCOL0,C:MOVE 0,0
180 FOR SIDE=0 TO S
190 MOVE 0,0:A=SIDE*2*PI/S
200 X(SIDE)=R*COSA:Y(SIDE)=R*SINA
210 PLOT85,R*COSA,R*SINA
220 NEXT SIDE
230 MOVE 0,0:PLOT85,R,0:GCOLRND(5)-1,RND(4)-1
240 FOR SIDE=1 TO S
250 FOR L=SIDE TO S
260 MOVE X(SIDE),Y(SIDE):DRAW X(L),Y(L):NEXT L
270 NEXT SIDE:VDU19,RND(4)-1,RND(8)-1,0,0,0:G=INKEY(250)
280 ENDPROC
```

8

Tuttle – a screen turtle

Don't let the shortness of this program fool you; many people will consider this to be the most exciting and creative program in the book and perhaps the most creative that they have seen for a long time. Briefly stated, it draws patterns on command. Having said that, however, we are a long way from realising its potential. Consider a polygon – any polygon – with any number of sides from three (a triangle) to say 30 (which will appear as a circle). Now a program that will accurately do that alone would be interesting enough, but this program does much more.

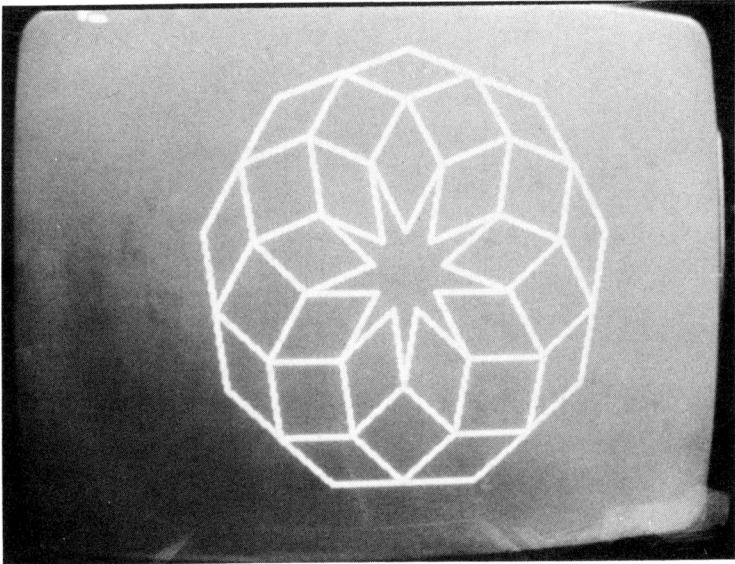

As an illustration imagine a six-sided figure, or hexagon. If we instruct the computer to draw only five sides of the six and then break away and start drawing another hexagon, it takes but little imagination to see that if the same rules are followed, a complex pattern will be produced that eventually assumes a symmetry and winds up where it started from. In the program, this is called a BLOCK.

Now suppose that upon completion of a block, the program breaks away yet again to draw another block – then another and another – and the most complex and beautiful patterns can emerge before once again the drawing point winds up where it started.

This is what the program does. In order to execute the design, the program needs to know (a) the number of sides of the base polygon, (b) the number of those sides it must draw before breaking away, (c) the regular length of side, (d) the angle that it must break away after drawing the part-polygon, and (e) the angle that it must break away after completing a block. In practice, (d) and (e) are best identical, so I have left them like that.

The turtle of my title? Well that comes about from LOGO and 'turtle graphics'. We may consider the drawing point as a turtle or some object capable of obeying instructions. At any time the turtle is not 'aware' of its position on the screen, but simply obeys two orders: go forward a certain distance, or turn through a certain angle. One remarkable thing about this program is that although the

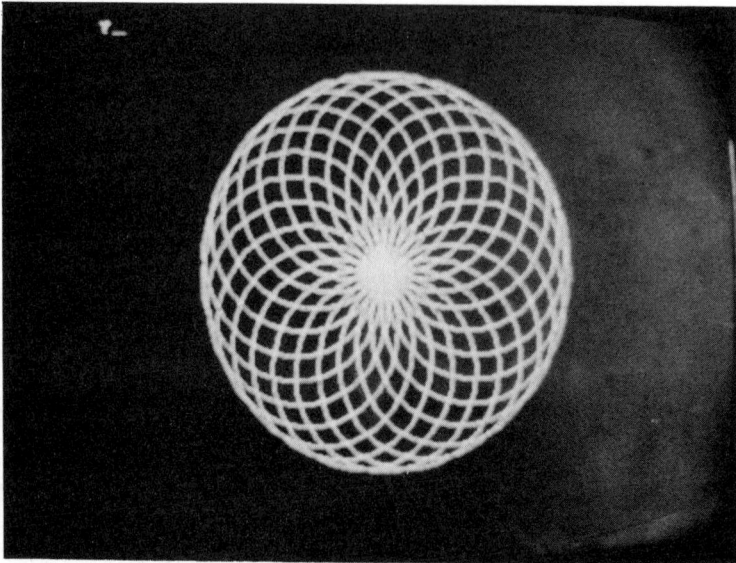

drawing point is calculated in this way – perhaps thousands of times – it executes the patterns without fault, precisely drawing over another line or through a particular point quite meticulously.

Unravelling the listing, the single polygon-drawing part is in lines 170 to 210, with the calculations for the sides taking place on lines 180 and 190. Line 200 is the only instruction-to-draw in the entire program. It will be seen that around that loop is another, with TURN counting the times through the loop. Hence a certain number of TURNs go to make up one BLOCK. Line 220 of course is the break-away calculation.

The program allows for either one block to be drawn (SINGLE) or several, equal to the number of sides on the basic polygon (MULTIPLE), so line 260 determines if we must stop or not after completion of a block. Line 140 is interesting. Consider our turtle again: it has come to the end of drawing a line and must now determine through how many radians it must turn before starting on its next line (see the diagram). Since this angle will be constant

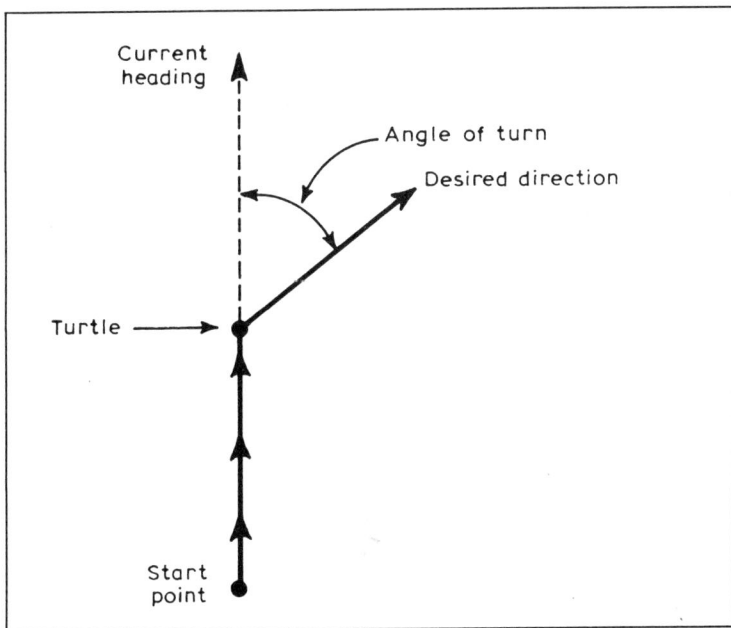

throughout the drawing process it need be calculated only once, on line 140.

When trying the program for the first time, enter responses as follows:

SIDES? 8
DRAWN? 7
ADD? 3
SIZE? (DEFAULT = 100)? (RETURN)
MULTIPLE OR SINGLE* (M-S)? (RETURN)

The screen will then clear and the pattern will be drawn immediately. It will be noticed that SIZE and SINGLE are default values, which means that you may press the RETURN key without typing anything. The ADD input is the number of angle increments to be added on break-away and of course a different value will produce a different pattern.

Sometimes the completed pattern may be either too big to fit onto the screen or else too small to distinguish and appreciate. This is where the SIZE input comes in, for by entering values greater or smaller than 100 one may expand or shrink the design.

When the design is completed, a question mark appears in the upper left corner – so as not to spoil the design – and one may appreciate the display for as long as one wishes. Pressing RETURN clears the screen ready for another design. If you have a printer capable of reproducing graphics, a screen dump routine would be marvellous for this program, and you could fill your study wall with beautiful computer-generated designs. Alternatively, tracing paper may be Sellotaped over the screen and the designs copied carefully. I suggest that one marks only the corners of patterns, joining up later with a good ruler and Indian ink. A pair of parallel rulers would be useful too. Children will love colouring the designs with crayon or paint, and it is a perfect activity when it is too cold or wet for them to play outside.

If you wish, you could alter the break-away angle after each block. Change line 240 to B=B+J*2*PI/S:MOVE X,Y and have another input for J at a new line 65.

```
 10 REM - Tuttle
 20 REM - A pattern-drawing screen turtle
 30 MODE7:ON ERROR GOTO270
 40 INPUT'''"SIDES",S
 50 INPUT"DRAWN",D
 60 INPUT"ADD",I
 70 INPUT"SIZE? (DEFAULT=100)",G$
 80 IF G$="" SIZE=100 ELSE SIZE=VAL(G$)
 85 REPEAT
 90 INPUT"MULTIPLE OR SINGLE* (M-S)",G$
100 UNTIL G$="M" OR G$="S" OR G$=""
110 IF G$="" G$="S"
130 MODE1:X=620:Y=510:GCOL0,2
140 B=I*2*PI/S:MOVE X,Y
150 BLOCK=0
160 FOR TURN=1 TO S
170 FOR SIDE=1 TO D
180 A=SIDE*2*PI/S:A=A+B
190 X1=SIZE*COSA:Y1=SIZE*SINA
200 PLOT1,X1,Y1
210 NEXT SIDE
220 B=B+I*2*PI/S
230 NEXT TURN
240 B=B+I*2*PI/S:MOVE X,Y
250 BLOCK=BLOCK+1
260 IF G$<>"S" AND BLOCK<=S GOTO160
270 INPUT G$:GOTO20
```

9

Score

The idea of Score is that every number from 1 to 10 must be scored, once and once only. The computer rolls two dice, and you decide how you want them scoring. For example, if the sum of the two dice is 8, you could score 8 alone, or 7 and 1, or 5 and 3, or 5, 2 and 1 . . . but you get the idea. The twin snags are that you *must* make up the dice-roll total, and that you cannot score any number twice. The result is an extraordinarily difficult game to win.

After the instructions, lines 100 to 130 draw ten score boxes and clear the array. Lines 180 to 220 draw two pretty boxes in which appear the dice rolls, and line 240 restricts communication texts to the lower portion of the screen. The fearsome line numbered 320 ensures that the chosen number – if legal – appears in the appropriate array box, so that at all times the user has the array before him and can see which numbers have not yet been scored. You are prevented from cheating, but the program is not intelligent enough to know when the player is in a 'no-win' situation. It is up to the user to recognise this and type '99' to concede the game. The screen will then clear and another game is started automatically.

Variables

A(10)	The array 1–10, each element of which has to be scored
Y%	Counter for box rows
X%	Box number in the row
X	General counter
D1	First dice roll
D2	Second dice roll
DICE	Sum of dice rolls as yet unscored

P	Player's input
FLAG	If = 1, an unscored array element found
X$	Title text
C%	Title text colour
L%	Length of box
H%	Height of box
F%	Box input flag
S%	Sound counter

```
  10 MODE7:PROCTITLE("SCORE")
  20 PRINT''' "In this game, you have to 'score' all"
  30 PRINT"numbers from 1 to 10. Two dice are used"
  40 PRINT"& if the roll is (eg) 8, you can score"
  50 PRINT"2 and 6, or 3 and 5, or 1, 2 and 5."
  60 PRINT'"You may not score any number twice, and"
  70 PRINT"you must always make up the total of"
  80 PRINT"the dice roll.":PROCRET
  90 DIM A(10)
 100 MODE7:FOR Y%=1 TO 2:FOR X%=0 TO 4
 110 PROCbox(X%*7,Y%*4,2,1,148,1)
 120 NEXT:NEXT
 130 FORX=1 TO 10:A(X)=0:NEXT
 140
 150 REM - Game loop
 160
 170 PRINTTAB(0,12);"Dice roll - "
 180 PROCbox(14,12,2,1,149,1)
 190 PROCbox(21,12,2,1,149,1)
 200 D1=RND(6):D2=RND(6)
 210 PRINTTAB(16,12);CHR$135;D1
 220 PRINTTAB(23,12);CHR$135;D2
 230 DICE=D1+D2
 240 VDU28,0,24,39,15
 250 CLS:PRINT"Which number(s) to score? Press RETURN"
 260 PRINT"after each. Type 99 to quit."
 270 INPUT P:IF P=99 GOTO100 ELSE IF P>10 GOTO250
 280 IF A(P)=0 GOTO300
 290 VDU7:PRINT"That number has been scored.":PROCRET:GOTO270
 300 IF DICE-P>=0 GOTO320 ELSE VDU7
 310 PRINT"That number is too big.":PROCRET:GOTO270
 320 VDU26:PRINTTAB((P-1)MOD5*7+2,((P-1)DIV5+1)*4);CHR$135;P
 330 VDU28,0,24,39,15
 340 A(P)=P:DICE=DICE-P
 350 IF DICE>0 CLS:PRINT"Next";:GOTO270
 360
 370 REM - Check for win
 380
 390 FLAG=0:FOR X=1 TO 10:IF A(X)=0 FLAG=1
 400 NEXT:CLS:IF FLAG=1 GOTO 420
 410 PROCDBL(5,15,131,"YOU WIN!"):PROCWARBLE:END
 420 PRINT"For next dice throw -":PROCRET:VDU26:GOTO170
```

```
425
430 DEFPROCTITLE(X$)
440 PRINTCHR$132;;STRING$(19,"Oo")
450 PROCDBL((36-LEN(X$))/2,4,131,X$)
460 PRINT''CHR$132;;STRING$(19,"Oo")
465 ENDPROC
466
470 DEFPROCDBL(X%,Y%,C%,X$)
480 PRINTTAB(X%,Y%);CHR$141;CHR$C%;X$
490 PRINTTAB(X%,Y%+1);CHR$141;CHR$C%;X$:ENDPROC
500
510 DEFPROCbox(X%,Y%,L%,H%,C%,F%)
520 LOCALV%,W%,I%,J%
530 PRINTTAB(X%,Y%);
540 V%=VPOS:W%=POS:PRINTTAB(W%,V%-H%);CHR$C%;"7";
550 FORI%=0TOL%+1:PRINT"£";:NEXT:PRINT"k"
560 PRINTTAB(W%,V%+1);CHR$C%;"u";
570 FORI%=0TOL%+1:PRINT"p";:NEXT:PRINT"z"
580 FORJ%=V%-H%+1TOV%:PRINTTAB(W%,J%);CHR$C%;"5":NEXT
590 FORJ%=V%-H%+1TOV%:PRINTTAB(W%+L%+3,J%);CHR$C%;"j"
600 NEXT:IF F%GOTO680
610 PRINTTAB(W%+2,V%);"";
620 FORI%=1TOL%:PRINT".";:NEXT
630 PRINTTAB(W%+3,V%);:X$=""
640 G$=GET$:IF ASCG$=13 GOTO680
650 IF ASCG$<>127 PRINT;G$;:X$=X$+G$:GOTO640
660 IF X$="" GOTO 640
670 X$=LEFT$(X$,1):PRINTCHR$8;".";CHR$8:GOTO640
680 ENDPROC
690
700 DEFPROCRET
710 PRINTTAB(5,22);"PressRETURN   ";:G$=GET$
720 ENDPROC
730
740 DEFPROCWARBLE
750 FORS%=1TO20:SOUND1,-12,30,1
760 SOUND1,-12,100,1:NEXT:ENDPROC
```

10

Greed

It's interesting to observe the tactics adopted by different people when playing this game. The computer rolls a dice (or die, if you insist) and asks if you want to roll again. The point is that the dice scores keep adding up for as long as you like, until a one is rolled, when the score is reduced to zero and play passes to the next player. However, if you drop out at any time, the score is retained and added to your total score. The player first reaching a total score of 200 is the winner. There is the cautious type of player who agonises over every decision; the dashing type who recklessly goes on rolling and rolling; and the super-cautious type who rarely rolls more than once, and never – but never – rolls three times. Perhaps we should call the game 'Caution'.

What should our tactics be? Taken over a long period of time, the dice will show an almost equal frequency of ones, twos, threes, etc., so strictly speaking, if we roll five times without showing a one, we ought to be satisfied. On the other hand . . .

Any number of players may take part. During the game the current player is addressed by name, so that no confusion may arise. On his turn, the player sees a labelled box with his overall score, another with his score this turn, one for the dice roll and, finally, a question asking if he wishes to roll again. Press Y (RETURN) or RETURN alone for another throw. Press N (RETURN) to retain the score.

Lines 50 to 70 accept the players' names and we go straight into the game. The listing should be quite self-explanatory and easy to follow, except perhaps for the reminder about the parameters that are passed to PROCbox. In order these are (1) position of box from left of screen, (2) position down from top of screen, (3) its length internally; i.e. number of characters it can hold, (4) its height internally, (5) its colour, and (6) whether or not an input is required.

Variables

PL%	Number of players
P%(X)	Total score for each player
P$(X)	Name of each player (maximum 12 characters)
X%	General counter
PLAYER%	Number of current player
SCORE%	Current score not yet secured
X$	Player input Y or N (or just RETURN)
DICE	Dice throw
W$	Dummy

```
 10 MODE7:PROCTITLE("GREED")
 20 INPUT''''"How many players",PL%:IF PL%>8 GOTO10
 30 DIM P%(PL%),P$(PL%)
 40 CLS:PRINT''"Please type your names"
 50 FOR X%=1 TO PL%:PRINT''"Player #";X%
 60 PROCbox(12,X%*2+3,12,1,148,0)
 70 P$(X%)=X$:NEXT
 80
 90 REM - Game loop
100
110 REPEAT
120 FOR PLAYER%=1 TO PL%
130 CLS:PROCTITLE(P$(PLAYER%)+"'S TURN")
140 PRINT''''"Score so far":PROCbox(15,11,3,1,148,1)
150 PRINTTAB(17,11);CHR$135;P%(PLAYER%);CHR$148
160 SCORE%=0
170
180 REM - Player's loop
190
200 PRINTTAB(0,14);"Score this turn"
210 PROCbox(15,14,3,1,148,1)
220 PRINTTAB(17,14);CHR$135;SCORE%;CHR$148
230 PRINTTAB(0,17);"Roll die (Y-N)?"
240 PROCbox(17,17,1,1,148,0)
250 IF X$<>"N" GOTO 290
260 P%(PLAYER%)=P%(PLAYER%)+SCORE%
270 IF P%(PLAYER%)>=200 GOTO 410
280 GOTO 370
290 DICE=RND(6)
300 PRINTTAB(0,19);"Roll"
310 PROCbox(17,19,1,1,148,1)
320 PRINTTAB(19,19);CHR$135;DICE;CHR$148
330 IF DICE=1 GOTO360
340 W$=INKEY$(300):SCORE%=SCORE%+DICE
350 PRINTTAB(20,19);" ":GOTO200
360 PRINT'"You lose.  Score this turn=0"
370 PROCRET:NEXT PLAYER%
380 UNTIL 0
```

```
390
400 REM - A winner
410
420 CLS:PROCDBL(0,5,129,P$(PLAYER%)+" WINS!")
430 END
440
450 DEFPROCTITLE(X$)
460 PRINTCHR$132;STRING$(19,"Oo")
470 PROCDBL((36-LEN(X$))/2,4,131,X$)
480 PRINTCHR$132;STRING$(19,"Oo")
490 ENDPROC
500
510 DEFPROCDBL(X%,Y%,C%,X$)
520 PRINTTAB(X%,Y%);CHR$141;CHR$C%;X$
530 PRINTTAB(X%,Y%+1);CHR$141;CHR$C%;X$
540 ENDPROC
550
560 DEFPROCbox(X%,Y%,L%,H%,C%,F%)
570 LOCALV%,W%,I%,J%
580 PRINTTAB(X%,Y%);
590 V%=VPOS:W%=POS
600 PRINTTAB(W%,V%-H%);CHR$C%;"7";
610 FORI%=0TOL%+1:PRINT"£";:NEXT
620 PRINT"k":PRINTTAB(W%,V%+1);CHR$C%;"u";
630 FORI%=0TOL%+1:PRINT"p";:NEXT:PRINT"z"
640 FORJ%=V%-H%+1TOV%:PRINTTAB(W%,J%);CHR$C%;"5":NEXT
650 FORJ%=V%-H%+1TOV%
660 PRINTTAB(W%+L%+3,J%);CHR$C%;"j":NEXT
670 IF F%GOTO750
680 PRINTTAB(W%+2,V%);"";
690 FORI%=1TOL%:PRINT".";:NEXT
700 PRINTTAB(W%+3,V%);:X$=""
710 G$=GET$:IF ASCG$=13 GOTO750
720 IF ASCG$<>127 PRINT;G$;:X$=X$+G$:GOTO710
730 IF X$="" GOTO 710 ELSE X$=LEFT$(X$,1)
740 PRINTCHR$8;".";CHR$8:GOTO710
750 ENDPROC
760
770 DEFPROCRET
780 PRINTTAB(5,23);CHR$131;"Press";
790 PRINTCHR$132;CHR$157;CHR$129;"RETURN  ";CHR$156;
800 G$=GET$:ENDPROC
```

11

Pakistani pool

This is a game that originated in Pakistan, where players gamble on the number of heads that will show when 25 coins are tossed. In this implementation, six players may take part. If no-one guesses correctly, all bets are retained in the pool for the next throw. All start with £10 and the game ends if any player is reduced to zero cash.

Names of players are collected and each given £10, and then in line 140 the game loop is entered. Each player is asked for his or her guess and then PROCTHROW is called 25 times, one for each coin. PROCTHROW shows H and T alternately for a little while before settling randomly for one or the other. After the throw, each player in turn is told the result of his or her bet and finally a check is made that all have some cash for the next round.

Variables

P$(6)	Array containing names of players
C%(6)	The cash state of each player
H%(6)	The number of heads that each player bets on
P%	Total number of players, 1 to 6
X%	General counter
H%	Number of heads thrown
T%	Number of tails thrown
F%	Flag; if 0, no player guessed correctly
POOL%	Cash held in pool
Z%	Spin count in coin tossing
W%	Dummy
C%	Colour of double-size print

```
10 REM - Pakistani Pool
20 DIM P$(6),C%(6),H%(6)
30 MODE7:PRINTSTRING$(19,"oO")
40 PROCDBL(10,5,130,"PAKISTANI POOL")
50 PRINT'''STRING$(19,"oO")
60 CLS:INPUT''"How many players (max 6)...?"P%
70 IF P%<1 OR P%>6 GOTO60
80 FOR X%=1 TO P%
90 PRINT''CHR$(128+X%);"Player #";X%;" -"
100 PRINT"What is your name ";
110 INPUT P$(X%):C%(X%)=10:NEXT:POOL%=0
120
130 CLS:REM - Game loop
140 FOR X%=1 TO P%
150 PRINT''CHR$(128+X%);P$(X%);
160 PRINT" - heads out of 25 ";:INPUT H%(X%):NEXT
170
180 REM - Coins tossed
190 CLS:PROCDBL(5,5,129,"THE THROW -")
200 PROCDBL(8,15,130,"HEADS    TAILS")
210 PRINTTAB(0,10);CHR$131;:H%=0:T%=0
220 FOR C%=2 TO 26:PROCTHROW:NEXT C%
230 PRINTTAB(15,21);"PRESS RETURN...";:INPUT Q$
235
240 REM - SETTLE BETS
250 F%=0:FOR X%=1 TO P%:CLS
260 PROCDBL(5,3,128+X%,P$(X%))
270 IF H%(X%)=H% GOTO330
280 PROCDBL(5,6,129,"LOST")
290 C%(X%)=C%(X%)-1
300 PRINT''"You have £";C%(X%);" left"
310 PRINT"Press RETURN...";:INPUT Q$
320 GOTO400
330 PROCDBL(5,6,131,"WON!")
340 IF POOL%=0 GOTO370
350 PRINT''CHR$133;"YOU SCOOP £";POOL%;" FROM THE POOL."
360 C%(X%)=C%(X%)+POOL%:POOL%=0
370 C%(X%)=C%(X%)+P%-1
380 PRINT''"You now have £";C%(X%)'
390 PRINT'"Press RETURN...";:INPUT Q$:F%=1
400 NEXT
410 REM - CHECK ALL HAVE CASH
420 Z%=0:FOR X%=1 TO P%:IF C%(X%)<=0 Z%=1
430 NEXT X%:IF Z%=0 GOTO460
440 CLS:PROCDBL(5,5,131,"FINAL SCORES")
450 FOR X%=1 TO P%:PRINTP$(X%);" - £";C%(X%):NEXT:END
455
460 REM - CHECK POOL
470 IF F%<>0 GOTO130
480 POOL%=POOL%+P%:CLS
490 PRINT''''CHR$129;"THERE IS £";POOL%;" IN THE POOL"
500 PRINTTAB(15,21);"PRESS RETURN...";:INPUT Q$
510 GOTO 130
520
530 DEFPROCTHROW
```

```
540 FOR Z%=1 TO 10
550 PRINTTAB(C%,10);"O":W%=INKEY(5):PRINTTAB(C%,10);"I"
560 W%=INKEY(5):NEXT Z%
570 PRINTTAB(C%,10);:IF RND(2)=2 PRINT"T":T%=T%+1:GOTO590
580 PRINT"H":H%=H%+1
590 S$=STR$H%+"          "+STR$T%
600 PROCDBL(10,18,130,S$)
610 ENDPROC
620 DEFPROCDBL(X%,Y%,C%,X$)
630 PRINTTAB(X%,Y%);CHR$C%;CHR$141;X$
640 PRINTTAB(X%,Y%+1);CHR$C%;CHR$141;X$:ENDPROC
```

12

Slide

This program is a computer implementation of those little plastic puzzles that you can buy, in which the user slides the pieces one at a time into the only available space. The object of the exercise is to arrange them in their natural order:

```
A   B   C   D
E   F   G   H
I   J   K   L
M   N   O
```

The advantage of this implementation over the plastic type is that every start condition is totally random and it is amazingly fast. Also, as a special dispensation, but only once per game, the user may swap any two letters, which is useful of course if you get into a situation you cannot see your way out of. Finally, the computer counts your moves and gives you a grading when – or if – you complete the puzzle.

Lines 30 and 40 determine the start condition, then lines 60 to 200 prepare the screen and print the puzzle, which appears as black letters on a white background, with a large red border. The instructions of line 80 appear in black on this border. Notice that there is no need to press RETURN after each move.

The game loop starts at line 120, so the computer is actually reprinting the puzzle after every move, but it is so fast that no delay is experienced and you can rattle the keys as fast as you are able. Notice too that although the puzzle is presented on a 4 × 4 square – a matrix, in the jargon – it is actually stored as a linear array, B%(1) to B%(16). After each move, the computer makes a swift check to see if you have won. It does this on lines 180–200. If the puzzle is not finished, on lines 210–250 it accepts a legal command only,

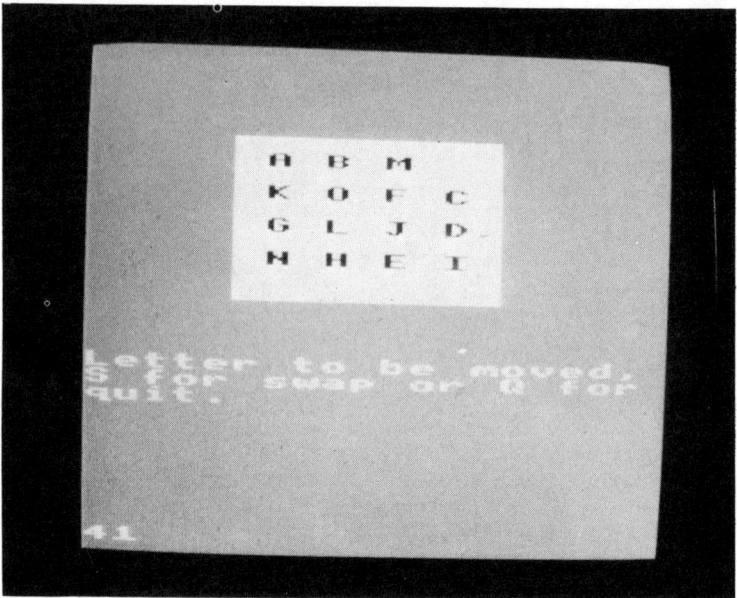

then checks to see if you can move the letter that you say that you wish to move. The rest of the program is fairly well annotated with REM statements, and it will be seen that the player grading takes place on lines 600–690.

Variables

B%(16)	The array for the letter and space positions
SWAP%	If 0, swap option has not yet been taken
M%	The count of moves
I%	General counter
J%	General counter
SPACE%	The position of the space
X%	General counter
A$	Command letter input by user
L%	ASCII value of letter to be moved
S$, T$	Two letters to be swapped

```
10 REM - Slide
20 DIM B%(16):SWAP%=0:M%=0:MODE7
30 FOR I%=65 TO 80
40 J%=RND(16):IF B%(J%)<>0 GOTO40 ELSE B%(J%)=I%
50 NEXT:SPACE%=J%
60 MODE5:GCOL0,129:CLG:COLOUR 131:GCOL0,2
70 VDU5:MOVE 0,400
80 PRINT"Letter to be moved, S for swap or Q for quit.":VDU4
90 REM - Define windows
100 VDU28,5,15,13,6,12,24,0;0;400;80;14
110 REM - Print puzzle
120 VDU4:COLOUR 0:PRINTTAB(1,1);
130 FOR X%=1 TO 16
140 IF B%(X%)=80 PRINT "  "; ELSE PRINT CHR$B%(X%);" ";
150 IF X% MOD 4=0 PRINT'" ";
160 NEXT:VDU5
170 REM - Check for solution
180 X%=1
190 IF B%(X%)<>X%+64 GOTO220
200 IF X%=15 GOTO570 ELSE X%=X%+1:GOTO190
210 REM - Get move
220 REPEAT:A$=GET$
230 UNTIL (A$>="A" AND A$<="O")OR A$="Q" OR A$="S"
240 IF A$="Q" THEN 520
250 IF A$="S" THEN 400
260 L%=ASC(A$):X%=1
270 IF B%(X%)<>L% X%=X%+1:GOTO270
280 REM - Check legality
290 IF ABS(SPACE%-X%)=4 GOTO370
300 IF ABS(SPACE%-X%)<>1 GOTO350
310 IF X%/4<>INT(X%/4) GOTO330
320 IF SPACE%=X%+1 GOTO350
330 IF (X%-1)/4<>INT((X%-1)/4) GOTO370
340 IF SPACE%<>X%-1 GOTO370
350 VDU7:GOTO220
360 REM - OK; swap
370 M%=M%+1:B%(X%)=80:B%(SPACE%)=L%:SPACE%=X%
380 VDU16:MOVE 0,50:PRINT;M%:GOTO120
390 REM - Swap option
400 IF SWAP%=1 VDU7:GOTO120
410 VDU24,0;0;1279;270;16:MOVE0,220
420 PRINT "Which 2 letters do  you want to swap?"
430 PRINT"(Press RETURN after each)"
440 INPUT S$,T$:I%=ASC(S$):J%=ASC(T$)
450 IFI%<65ORI%>79ORJ%<65ORJ%>79ORI%=J%VDU7,16:GOTO420
460 REM - Find and swap
470 X%=1:Y%=1
480 IF B%(X%)<>I% X%=X%+1:GOTO480
490 IF B%(Y%)<>J% Y%=Y%+1:GOTO490
500 B%(X%)=J%:B%(Y%)=I%
510 SWAP%=1:GCOL0,129:VDU16,24;0;0;400;80;:GOTO120
520 MODE7
521 PRINTTAB(5,10);"You quit the game after ";M%;" moves."
530 PRINT''"Do you want another game (Y-N)?";
```

```
540 REPEAT:G$=GET$:UNTIL G$="Y" OR G$="N"
550 IF G$="N"PRINT'''" G O O D B Y E":END
560 M%=0:SWAP%=0:FORX%=1 TO 16:B%(X%)=0:NEXT:GOTO30
570 MODE7:PRINTTAB(3,5);"C O N G R A T U L A T I O N S !"
580 FOR X%=1 TO 10:FOR Y%=50 TO 150
582 SOUND 17,-15,Y%,2:NEXT:NEXT
590 PRINT'''"You solved the problem in ";M%;" moves!"
600 IF M%<75 PRINT"You're a genius!":GOTO530
610 IF M%<100 PRINT"Absolutely brilliant!":GOTO530
620 IF M%<125 PRINT"Tremendous!":GOTO530
630 IF M%<150 PRINT"Excellent!":GOTO530
640 IF M%<175 PRINT"Very good!":GOTO530
650 IF M%<200 PRINT"Good!":GOTO530
660 IF M%<250 PRINT"Not bad.":GOTO530
670 IF M%<300 PRINT"Pretty fair.":GOTO530
680 IF M%<400 PRINT"Not very good, I'm afraid.":GOTO530
690 PRINT"Why don't you take up knitting?":GOTO530
```

13

Get that bird!

If your kids are like the one that has the contract to hike mud into our house, they will love a certain cartoon character that travels at a great rate of knots along a road, always eluding the foxy type who is trying to catch him. In this computer game, they are trying to catch the bird. We suppose that a charge of dynamite has been placed in the road and as soon as the bird appears, the player has to slap any key to detonate the charge. The problem is of course that the bird travels very fast indeed. Actually, I have included skill levels from 0

to 9, and although anyone can win at the lowest level, quite frankly I think that level 9 is completely impossible – which is to admit that I at least have never won at that level!

The background to the picture comprises sky and hills and contains a random element so that every game is slightly different. When you are tired of playing the game, you can try experimenting with the numeric values of line 90 in order to see the different types of terrain that will occur. What I have done is to divide the screen across into 12 sections and then, starting at the top of the picture, to create random values varying slightly as we move across. These are put into one row of the landscape array, L%(X,Y). Subsequent rows have a smaller deviation, so that the hills gently flatten into undulating land.

The road is always the same and is built around a sine wave decaying as it nears the bottom of the screen. In addition, choosing a step size of −43 (lines 210 and 250) makes it impossible for the road to follow the wave closely, thus appearing asymmetrical.

Lines 280 to 310 define four separate characters. These are four round shapes of increasing size, to represent the fleeting bird as it rushes headlong down the picture. In run-time, there is no opportunity to study the bird, and the general impression of something rushing down the road towards the viewer is quite sufficient. If desired however, the last two shapes might be redesigned as a cartoon character.   '

The game loop is contained in the REPEAT–UNTIL loop of lines 350 to 470 and will repeat forever until the player is successful. There is an indefinite pause in line 360 and then line 370 starts a cackling sound that accompanies the bird. The *FX15 command of line 360 has flushed the input buffer so that the user cannot slap a key before this instant. Line 390 closely mirrors the road construction, so the path of the bird is down the road centre, with lines 400 to 430 choosing a character size to suit the position down the screen.

Line 440 looks for a user input (no RETURN necessary), while line 450 checks if the bird has reached the bottom of the screen. The difficulty level affects the height up the screen that represents safety for the bird, with zero equal to the very bottom. This is checked on line 460. If a key has been hit and the bird is still above the safety level, the program jumps to line 510, where an explosive sound is made and a flashing explosion appears at an appropriate spot in the road.

Of the two procedures, PROCW provides a delay of three one-hundredths of a second for the reason outlined in the Bicycle Wheel program – the image of the spot or bird must be allowed to form before being wiped. A value less than three may make the bird

totally invisible, while a larger value will make the game a trifle too
easy. Try it and see. PROCPAINT will draw and fill any four-sided
figure by utilising two triangles. The colour is specified before the
procedure is called. Notice that we have a number of variables
declared as LOCAL; this is a useful provision, because not only may
we use the same variable labels elsewhere, but also there is a saving
in memory space, which sometimes is important.

Variables

L%(X,Y)	Landscape heights
LVL%	Difficulty level
Z%	Counter for row in landscape array
X%	Position along the row; also horizontal position
F%	Field counter
C1%	Field colour
Y%	Road sections, or vertical position
K	Timer for starting run; also check for key-pressed condition
Q%	Counter for decreasing amplitude of explosion (decay)

```
 10 DIML%(7,11):*FX9,0
 20 MODE7:PRINTTAB(5,5);"GET THAT BIRD!"'''
 30 PRINT"Difficulty level 0-9?"
 40 REPEAT:LVL%=GET-48:UNTIL LVL%>=0 AND LVL%<=9
 50
 60 REM - Draw background
 70
 80 MODE2:FOR Z%=1TO6
 90 Y%=RND(30)+(900-30*Z%):L%(Z%,1)=Y%
100 FOR X%=2 TO 11:IF RND(1)>.5 GOTO120
110 Y%=Y%+RND(20)/Z%
120 Y%=Y%-RND(20)/Z%
130 L%(Z%,X%)=Y%:NEXT:NEXT:GCOL0,134:CLG
14  FORF%=1TO6:READC1%:GCOL0,C1%:PROCpaint(F%):NEXTF%
150 ENVELOPE1,1,-26,-36,-45,255,255,255,127,0,0,-127,126,0
160 DATA4,5,2,3,2,3
170
180 REM - Draw road
190
200 VDU29,600;0;18,0,5:MOVE0,820:PLOT0,0,0:GCOL0,0
210 FOR Y%=820 TO 0 STEP-43
220 X%=SINY%*Y%*.6
230 PLOT85,(X%+820-Y%),Y%:PLOT81,-820+Y%,0
240 NEXT:GCOL0,7:MOVE0,820
```

```
250 FOR Y%=820 TO 0 STEP-43
260 DRAWSINY%*Y%*.6+(820-Y%)*.5,Y%:NEXT
270 GCOL4,0:*FX11,0
280 VDU5,23,224,192,192,0,0,0,0,0,0
290 VDU23,225,192,192,192,192,0,0,0,0
300 VDU23,226,224,224,224,224,224,224,0,0
310 VDU23,227,28,62,255,255,255,255,62,28
320
330 REM - Game loop
340
350 REPEAT
360 K=TIME:REPEAT:UNTIL TIME>=K+RND(1000)+300:*FX15,0
370 SOUND1,1,255,255
380 Y%=820:*FX12,0
390 X%=SINY%*Y%*.6+(820-Y%)*.5:MOVEX%,Y%:*FX15,1
400 IFY%<=200PRINTCHR$227:PROCW:PRINTCHR$227:GOTO440
410 IFY%<=400PRINTCHR$226:PROCW:PRINTCHR$226:GOTO440
420 IFY%<=600PRINTCHR$225:PROCW:PRINTCHR$225:GOTO440
430 PRINTCHR$224:PROCW:PRINTCHR$224
440 K=INKEY(0)
450 Y%=Y%-43:IFY%>=0 AND K=-1 GOTO390
460 IFLVL%*50<Y%GOTO510
465 *FX15,0
470 UNTIL 0
480
490 REM - Got him!
500
510 VDU29,X%+600;Y%+43;
520 FOR Z%=1 TO 10:MOVE0,0
530 MOVERND(200)-100,RND(200)
540 PLOT81,RND(200)-100,RND(200)
550 NEXT:*FX15,0
560 FOR Q%=-160TO0:SOUND0,Q%/10,6,1:NEXT
570 G$=INKEY$(400):MODE7
580 PRINTTAB(5,5);"YOU GOT HIM!"
590 G$=INKEY$(500):RESTORE:GOTO80
600
610 DEFPROCW:K=INKEY(3):MOVEX%,Y%:ENDPROC
620
630 DEFPROCpaint(S%):LOCALZ%,X%,X1%,A%,B%,C%,D%
640 FOR Z%=1 TO 10:X%=(Z%-1)*128:X1%=Z%*128
650 A%=L%(S%+1,Z%):B%=L%(S%+1,Z%+1)
660 C%=L%(S%,Z%):D%=L%(S%,Z%+1)
670 MOVE X%,A%:MOVE X%,C%
680 PLOT85,X1%,B%:PLOT85,X1%,D%
690 NEXT
700 ENDPROC
```

14

Torpedo run

Here is a great game for those who like shooting games. We suppose the player to be torpedo officer or captain of a warship. He has three torpedo tubes numbered left to right, each with a magazine of nine torpedoes. An infinite array of enemy ships is constantly parading from right to left of the screen. These are of different types, proceeding at different speeds at different distances up the screen. The player simply presses the numeric key 1, 2 or 3 according to which torpedo tube he wishes to fire. The track of the torpedo is then seen progressing up the screen until it either hits a

ship or disappears over the horizon. Only one torpedo may be in
motion at once and of course the player cannot fire more than the
specified nine torpedoes from each tube. At all times there is a
visual indication of how many torpedoes remain for each tube, and
of the player's score.

Scoring depends entirely upon difficulty. That is to say, the
leftmost torpedo tube (if successful) scores less than the rightmost.
Similarly, slower and larger targets score less than swift small ones,
and targets crossing near the bottom of the screen score less than
those on the horizon. Thus the game is a real test of skill. The game
ends when the player runs out of torpedoes, and the computer
retains details of the best six scores and their scorers.

Lines 30 and 40 draw the sea and the sky, then line 50 clears a
space at the bottom for text. Line 60 draws a white area to represent
the warship's foredeck. Lines 70 to 170 redefine graphic characters
that go to make up the five target ships, assembled in lines 180 to
220. Lines 240 to 270 draw the three torpedo tubes and print the
game conditions, number of torpedoes left, and score. The variable
D% is a flag that indicates whether or not a torpedo is running.

The game loop is now entered, and a target ship is chosen
randomly, also its velocity and its height up the screen. C% is its
appropriate background colour; normally green, but blue if it is on
the horizon. Lines 350 to 370 move the ship and, if a torpedo is not
running, line 390 checks to see if the player has fired by pressing 1,
2 or 3. The legality is checked on line 400. The next line checks to
see if there are still torpedoes available for the chosen tube and if so
the following lines decrement the count and launch the torpedo.

The BBC BASIC isn't very happy with TORP as a variable name,
so I have changed it to SHELLS. Lines 470 and 480 move the
torpedo track, which is simply a lengthening line extending up-
wards from the torpedo tube.

The end of the torpedo run is signalled when it encounters a
colour other than green. This is the POINT command of lines 480
and 500. A POINT colour of 2 is equivalent to green; 0 is black (a
target), and 6 is light blue (cyan), or the sky. Line 520 calculates the
score for each hit, and line 550 gives an explosive sound for a hit.
Lines 550 to 570 remove the stricken ship, with a little bit of sound
to accompany it.

If not hit, the ship continues to move off left and then in line 620
we check to see if the player has expended all of his torpedoes,
when that part of the game ends. The final score is given in line 630
and then lines 640 to 650 check if the score is in the best six so far
recorded. If so, the user is invited to type his name. The list of the
best six scores is given after every game and then line 730 starts
afresh.

Variables

S$(5)	Strings for target ships graphics
T%(3)	Torpedoes remaining for each of three tubes
B%(6)	Highest six scores, in order
B$(6)	Names of highest scorers
SHELLS	Total number of torpedoes expended
SC%	Running total of current score
X	General counter
X%	General counter. Also used for tracking target across screen
D%	Torpedo flag, where 0 = no torpedo running
F%	User input, 1, 2 or 3
S%	Number of current target, 1 to 5
V%	Fine-tuning to velocity of current target
Y%	Height up screen of current target
J%	Height of current torpedo
I%	Position across screen of current torpedo
Q%	Counter for explosion frequency and duration
C%	Background colour for target ship

```
 10 MODE7:PROCTITLE("TORPEDO RUN"):PROCRET
 20 DIMS$(5),T%(3),B%(6),B$(6):B%(1)=0
 30 MODE2:VDU24,0;812;1279;1023;18,0,134,16
 40 VDU26,24,0;0;1279;816;18,0,130,16
 50 VDU26,28,1,31,18,29
 60 MOVE64,0:MOVE1215,0:PLOT85,612,200
 70 VDU23,224,2,2,2,2,2,2,255,127,63
 80 VDU23,225,0,0,0,0,0,255,255,255
 90 VDU23,226,0,0,100,116,127,255,255,254
100 VDU23,227,0,0,6,118,118,127,255,255
110 VDU23,228,0,0,0,0,128,255,255,254
120 VDU23,229,0,0,0,60,12,255,127,63
130 VDU23,230,0,0,204,236,236,255,255,255
140 VDU23,231,0,0,0,0,0,255,255,254
150 VDU23,232,0,0,0,0,0,255,127,63
160 VDU23,233,0,0,62,124,124,255,255,255
170 VDU23,234,0,0,0,1,2,254,127,63
180 S$(1)=CHR$234+CHR$231
190 S$(2)=CHR$232+CHR$233
200 S$(3)=CHR$229+CHR$230+CHR$231
210 S$(4)=CHR$224+CHR$227+CHR$228
220 S$(5)=CHR$224+CHR$225+CHR$226
230 SHELLS=0:SC%=0:FORX=1TO3:T%(X)=9:NEXT:VDU5
240 GCOL0,0:FOR X%=300 TO 900 STEP 300
250 MOVE X%,0:MOVE X%+20,0:PLOT85,X%,220
260 PLOT 85,X%+20,220:NEXT
```

```
270 VDU4:CLS:PRINTTAB(3,0);"9   9   9"''"SCORE";
280 VDU5:D%=0
290
300 REM - Game loop
310
320 REPEAT
330 S%=RND(5):V%=RND(6)-1
340 Y%=RND(560)+350:IFY%>816 Y%=840
350 IF Y%=840 C%=6 ELSE C%=2
360 FOR X%=1150 TO -50 STEP -20+S%*2
370 MOVE X%,Y%:GCOL2,0:PRINT S$(S%)
380 IF D% GOTO470
390 F%=INKEY(S%):IF F%=-1 GOTO600
400 IF F%<>49ANDF%<>50ANDF%<>51GOTO600
410 F%=F%-48:IF T%(F%)<=0 GOTO600
420 VDU4:COLOUR0:PRINTTAB(F%*5-2,0);T%(F%)
430 T%(F%)=T%(F%)-1:COLOUR1:D%=1
440 PRINTTAB(F%*5-2,0);T%(F%):VDU5
450 I%=F%*300+10:J%=224
460 REM - Torpedo
470 GCOL0,7:MOVE I%,224:PLOT5,I%,J%
480 J%=J%+10:IF POINT(I%,J%)=2 GOTO600
490 SHELLS=SHELLS+1:D%=0:GCOL0,2
500 DRAW I%,224:IF POINT(I%,J%)<>0 GOTO600
510 REM - A hit
520 VDU4:SC%=SC%+(6-S%)*V%*F%+Y%/2
530 COLOUR3:PRINTTAB(6,2);SC%;:VDU5
540 FOR Q%=-160TO10STEP3:SOUND0,Q%/10,6,1:NEXT
550 GCOL0,C%:FORS%=Y%-32TOY%STEP4
560 SOUND1,-10,S%/4,1
570 MOVE0,S%:DRAW1239,S%:NEXT S%
580 X%=-100:GOTO610
590 REM - Move ship
600 GCOL1,C%:MOVE X%,Y%:PRINTS$(S%)
610 NEXT
620 UNTIL SHELLS=27:MODE7
630 PROCTITLE("FINAL SCORE "+STR$(SC%)):F%=1
640 IFSC%>B%(F%)GOTO660
650 F%=F%+1:IF F%<=6 GOTO640 ELSE 710
660 PRINTTAB(0,8);"Great score!":*FX15,1
670 INPUT"Please type your name",X$
680 FOR X=6 TO F% STEP-1
690 B$(X)=B$(X-1):B%(X)=B%(X-1):NEXT
700 B$(F%)=X$:B%(F%)=SC%
710 CLS:PROCTITLE("BEST SCORES TODAY")
720 PRINT''':FORX=1 TO6:PRINTB$(X);TAB(20);B%(X):NEXT
730 PROCRET:GOTO30
740 DEFPROCTITLE(X$)
750 PRINTCHR$132;STRING$(19,"Oo")
760 PROCDBL((36-LEN(X$))/2,3,131,X$)
770 PRINT'CHR$132;STRING$(19,"Oo")
780 ENDPROC
790
800 DEFPROCDBL(X%,Y%,C%,X$)
```

```
810 PRINTTAB(X%,Y%);CHR$141;CHR$C%;X$
820 PRINTTAB(X%,Y%+1);CHR$141;CHR$C%;X$
830 ENDPROC
840
850 DEFPROCRET
860 PRINTTAB(5,19);CHR$131;"Press";
870 PRINTCHR$132;CHR$157;CHR$129;"RETURN ";CHR$156;
880 G$=GET$:ENDPROC
```

15

Series

If we examine the number series 1,2,3,4,5,6 we can confidently predict that the next in line will be 7. What have we done? We have looked at the interval between the first number and the second and noted that it is 1. We have also looked at the next interval and noted that that too is 1. From that we hypothesise that all intervals will be 1. We go along the line checking this hypothesis and on finding it to be true, we extrapolate. We add 1 to the last, making 7.

Now consider 2,3,5,8,12,17 – what will be next? The first interval is 1; the second interval is 2. Mmmmm – perhaps the interval increases by 1 each time? Checking, we see that it does. The last interval is 5, so the next will be 6, making the next number in the series 23.

What about 78,9,77,10,76,11,75? Here it does not take much observation to see that there are two series interleaved; one going down; the other going up. Such series are often difficult to spot, as in 3,7,6,4,8,1,9, which again has two interleaved series. One decreases by 3 every time, while the other proceeds on a decaying increment – 3,6,8,9 – and will continue 9,8,6,3,–1.

When we turn to letters the same holds true, as in B,D,F,G,I or W,V,T,Q,M – the next are K and H respectively. In the case of letters however, the alphabet does not go on indefinitely in both directions, so there must be a wrap-around at each end, which is to say that A and Z are considered to be adjacent.

Now a computer program designed to produce series would not be very successful if it turned out only one or two types. Users would apply simple rules or tests and rapidly decipher the series. Not much fun there! However, fun and puzzling increase rapidly if a number of different types of series is available, as in the program listed. The user has a choice of numbers or letters; although the latter offer fewer types of series, most people find them more difficult. I won't explain the series types any further, but will leave you the opportunity to enjoy puzzling them out for yourself. Suffice to say that some series expect you to forecast only one number or letter, while some expect two. If your guess(es) are wrong, the computer will tell you what the answer should have been – and even then it is guaranteed that sometimes you will remain puzzled. Enjoy yourself!

The puzzle series is printed in white on a dark blue background, and if you are correct, a flashing 'RIGHT!' appears, with your score so far. If you are wrong, or press RETURN without an input, a 'WRONG' message appears, together with the answer. You are given ten problems and then a percentage score. If you elect to play again, totals and percentages are carried over to another ten problems.

Variables

R$	String to print to start a line in red
B$	Ditto in blue
R%	Record of correct answers
ALL%	Total number of problems attempted
G%	User's choice, 1 or 2
D%	Difficulty level
PROB%	Number of current problem
T%	Major type of series
A,B,C,D,E,F	Used for creation of different series
Z%	Numeric value of input guess
I%, J%	Ditto for twin inputs

```
 10 R$=CHR$129+CHR$157+CHR$135
 20 B$=CHR$132+CHR$157+CHR$135
 30 R%=0:ALL%=10
 40 MODE7:PROCDBL(12,2,"SERIES"):PRINTTAB(13);"           "''
 50 PRINT'"Do you want -"TAB(5,12);R$;TAB(30);CHR$156
 60 PRINTTAB(5,13);R$;"(1) Numbers   ";CHR$156
 70 PRINTTAB(5,14);R$;"(2) Letters   ";CHR$156
 80 PRINTTAB(5,15);R$;"              ";CHR$156
 90 PRINT'''CHR$131;"Your choice.....?";
100 REPEAT:G%=GET-48:UNTIL G%=1 OR G%=2
110 PRINTG%:IF G%=2 D%=0:GOTO150
120 PRINT''"How difficult?  Choose a number"''
130 PRINT"from 1 (easy) to 4 (hard)...";
140 REPEAT:D%=GET:UNTIL D%>48 AND D%<54:D%=D%-48:PRINT;D%
150 FOR PROB%=1TO10:PROCNUM:CLS:PRINT'''
```

```
160 ON G% GOTO170,310
170 T%=RND(D%+3)
180 ON T%GOSUB460,500,550,590,610,660,730
190 NEXT
200 MODE7:PRINTTAB(0,3);R$'R$"          S C O R E"
210 PRINTR$;"                        "
220 PRINTR$"You scored ";R%;" out of ";ALL%
230 PRINTR$"(or ";R%*100/ALL%;"%)"
240 PRINTR$R$'''"Do you want to play again (Y-N)?"
250 REPEAT:G$=GET$:UNTIL G$="Y" OR G$="N"
260 IFG$="Y"CLS:ALL%=ALL%+10:GOTO40
270 PRINTR$'R$"  G O O D B Y E"'R$:END
280
290 REM - LETTERS
300
310 IFA=0 A=26
320 IFB=0 B=1
330 ONRND(3)GOTO340,370,400
340 PRINTB$;:FOR X%=1 TO 6:PRINT;CHR$(A+64);"  ";
350 A=(A+B):A=A MOD 26:IF A=0 A=26
360 NEXT:PROCKID(A):GOTO190
370 PRINTB$;:FOR X%=1 TO 6:PRINT;CHR$(A+64);"  ";
380 A=(A-B):IF A<=0 A=26+A
390 NEXT:PROCKID(A):GOTO190
400 PRINTB$;:FOR X%=1 TO 6:PRINT;CHR$(A+64);"  ";
410 A=A+B:B=B+1:A=A MOD 26:IF A=0 A=26
420 NEXT:PROCKID(A):GOTO340
430
440 REM - NUMBERS
450
460 PRINT;B$;:FOR X%=1 TO 6
470 PRINT;B+X%*A;"  ";:NEXT
480 PROCKID(7*A+B)
490 RETURN
500 IF RND(1)>.5 C=1 ELSE C=-1
510 PRINT;B$;:FOR X%=1 TO 6
520 PRINT;B;"  ";:B=B+A:A=A+C:NEXT
530 PROCKID(B)
540 RETURN
550 PRINT;B$;:FOR X%=1 TO 4
560 PRINT;A+X%*C;"  ";B+X%*D;"  ";:NEXT
570 PROCMORE(A+5*C,B+5*D)
580 RETURN
590 D=-D:GOTO550
600 RETURN
610 I%=RND(7)
620 PRINT;B$;:FOR X%=1 TO 4
630 PRINT;A;" ";B;"  ";C;"  ";:A=A+I%:B=B+I%:C=C+I%
640 NEXT:PROCMORE(A,B)
650 RETURN
660 IF RND(1)>.5 E=1 ELSE E=-1
670 IF RND(1)>.5 F=1 ELSE F=-1
680 PRINT;B$;:FOR X%=1 TO 5
690 PRINT;A;" ";B;"  ";
700 A=A+C:B=B+D:C=C+E:D=D+F:NEXT
710 PROCMORE(A,B)
```

```
 720 RETURN
 730 ON RND(3) GOTO 740,770,810
 740 A=RND(4):PRINT;B$;:FOR X%=1 TO 5
 750 PRINT;A;"   ";:A=A*2:NEXT:PROCKID(A)
 760 RETURN
 770 A=RND(6):PRINT;B$;:FOR X%=1 TO 5
 780 PRINT;A*A;"   ";:A=A+1:NEXT:PROCKID(A*A)
 790 RETURN
 800 REM - SUMS
 810 PRINT;B$;:FOR X%=1 TO 5
 820 PRINT;"";:C=A:A=B:B=A+C:NEXT:PROCKID(A)
 830 RETURN
 840
 850 DEFPROCRT
 860 R%=R%+1:PRINT''B$
 870 PRINT;B$;CHR$136;"R I G H T !   (Your score=";R%;")"
 880 PRINT B$
 890 ENDPROC
 900
 910 DEFPROCWRONG(Q%)
 920 PRINT''R$
 930 PRINTR$;"SORRY - THAT IS NOT RIGHT"
 940 PRINTR$
 950 PRINTR$;"THE CORRECT ANSWER IS ";
 960 IF G%=1 PRINT Q% ELSE PRINT CHR$(Q%+64)
 970 PRINTR$
 980 ENDPROC
 990
1000 DEFPROCNUM
1010 A=RND(10+D%)-7:B=RND(10+D%)-7:C=RND(10+D%)-7:
     D=RND(10+D%)-7
1020 IF D%<=2 A=ABS(A):B=ABS(B):C=ABS(B):D=ABS(D)
1030 ENDPROC
1040
1050 DEFPROCKID(Q%)
1060 PRINT'''CHR$131;"What comes next?....";:INPUT Z$
1070 IF G%=2 Z%=ASC(Z$)-64 ELSE Z%=VAL(Z$)
1080 IF Z%=Q% PROCRT:GOTO1100
1090 PROCWRONG(Q%)
1100 PROCRET:ENDPROC
1110
1120 DEFPROCRET
1130 PRINT''CHR$129;"Press RETURN when ready....";
1140 Q$=GET$:CLS:ENDPROC
1150
1160 DEFPROCMORE(I%,J%)
1170 PRINT'''CHR$131;"What comes next?....";:INPUT Z%
1180 IF Z%<>I% PROCWRONG(I%):GOTO1210
1190 PRINT''CHR$131;"And after that?...";:INPUT Z%
1200 IF Z%<>J% PROCWRONG(J%) ELSE PROCRT
1210 PROCRET:ENDPROC
1220
1230 DEFPROCDBL(X%,Y%,X$)
1240 PRINTTAB(X%,Y%);CHR$141;X$
1250 PRINTTAB(X%,Y%+1);CHR$141;X$
1260 ENDPROC
```

16

Word squares

Another firm favourite with children! In fact, the one in our house used to buy whole books of these problems every week until I wrote this program.

You can either enter your own choice of words for the kids to find, or they can have the computer choose words from a series of DATA statements – see lines 990 to 1070. You could put your own words in here, but memory space is rather tight and you cannot extend the number of words very much before getting a 'No room' message at run time. This is because of the graphics mode used, and a useful alteration – if you have a printer – would be to have the puzzle printed out on paper rather than on the screen, which would result in an enormous saving of memory.

The first screen page asks if you wish to enter your own words. Type Y or N as appropriate. If you enter your own words, you must type 18 words, each of ten letters or less, pressing RETURN after each one. This is taken care of in PROCWORDSIN, and there is no check for duplicates. If you choose to have the computer use its own words, simply type N.

The computer now displays the word 'WORKING . . .' for a few seconds as it fits the words into the square – actually a rectangle, 19 characters wide by 9 high. Words are fitted in any direction – forwards, backwards, up, down or diagonally – and then the rest of the rectangle is filled with junk characters. The result is printed on the screen in white lower case, a part of the program automatically converting any upper-case letters. Beneath the white display is a ruled line in red and a list of all words that have been fitted into the square. There may be gaps in this list, representing words that have been tried 25 times without success. (Alter this if you like in line 640, but don't have it try too many times or you may sit around for a long time waiting for the puzzle.)

Beneath the list is the single prompt, 'Word?' The user now sits and stares at the matrix, trying to spot one of the embedded words. When one has been seen, he or she types the whole word – spelling correctly – and presses RETURN. Now we must check that they have the right word (not just guessing) and to this end the user must enter two numbers, (a) the ROW of the initial letter (counting down from the top), and (b) the COLUMN (counting from the left).

If wrong, an appropriate message is printed, but if right, both the word in the array and the word in the list are overprinted in yellow, which is a great aid. Play continues in this way until either the user types the whole word 'QUIT' or completes the puzzle by finding every word listed. The computer then prints out the time taken in minutes. If the player has quit, the solution is highlighted; every junk letter is removed from the screen. A new game may then be restarted by typing RUN.

Turning to the listing, words to be fitted into the puzzle are entered into the array W$(18), either from the keyboard in PROC-WORDSIN or from the DATA statements, chosen in lines 150 to 180. In the latter case, duplicates are checked for and eliminated by lines 170 and 180.

PROCFIT of course fits the words into the matrix, each word taken in turn and given 25 tries before being blanked and ignored (line 640). When making a try, the computer randomly picks a starting position and direction in line 650, reading the appropriate movement vectors from the DATA line 980 into I% and J%· Then it makes a trial fit, incrementing the position according to the vectors. If the array at that point is empty or contains the same letter, fitting can proceed (line 670), but fitting stops if the edge of the matrix is met or the other conditions are not (line 680). If the trial fit is satisfactory, lines 710 to 740 actually place the word. When all words have been dealt with, lines 780 to 800 fill up the rest of the array with junk letters.

Back in the main program, the game loop is entered. This part of the program should be self-explanatory. The user inputs his or her detected word, its row and its column. A call to PROCLCASE translates any upper-case letters and then the computer checks (lines 290 to 310) first to see if the word is contained in the puzzle. It then reads the array D%(X,Y), where the X,Y start of the word has been stored, and its direction vector. Lines 400 and 410 overprint the word in the puzzle, with line 420 overprinting the same word in the list of words to find. WIN is the number of words found and if this matches DONE – the number of words fitted – the puzzle has been solved completely. Lines 460 to 480 wipe off the junk letters, revealing the solution.

Variables

C$	User's choice, Y = own words, N = computer's
W$(18)	18 words to be fitted
D%(X,Y)	Details of where each word is in puzzle, where
	X = number of word
	Y = 1 = X co-ordinate
	2 = Y co-ordinate
	3 = Direction vector, 1 to 8
A$(19,9)	Displayed array, including junk
B$(19,9)	Solution array
L$	20 underscores for a straight line rule
W$	Current input word
Y%	Random number to pick a word from DATA
Z$	Chosen word
FLAG	Flag for duplicates
T%	Counter when searching for duplicate
TIME	Computer's internal elapsed-time clock
WIN	Number of words correctly identified
R%	User's input for row
C%	User's input for column
WN%	Word number
X%	General counter
I%, J%	Movement vectors

Y$ Lower-case version of W$
DONE   Number of words fitted
X$ Message string
TRY   Number of attempts at fitting
X1%, Y1% Co-ordinates while attempting fit
L%   Letters successfully tried

```
 10 REM - Word square
 20 MODE7:PROCDBL(5,3,131,"WORD SQUARE")
 30 PRINT''"Do you want to put in your own words (Y-N)?"
 40 REPEAT:C$=GET$:UNTILC$="Y"ORC$="N"
 50 DIMW$(18),D%(18,3),A$(19,9),B$(19,9)
 60 L$=STRING$(20," ")
 70 IFC$<>"Y"GOTO130
 80 PRINT''"Please type 18 words of not more than"
 90 PRINT"10 letters each."':PROCWORDSIN
100
110 REM - Fit words into rectangle
120
130 CLS:PROCDBL(5,5,131,"WORKING....")
140 IFC$="Y"GOTO190
150 FORW%=1TO18
155 RESTORE 990
160 Y%=RND(65):FORZ%=1TOY%:READZ$:NEXT
170 FLAG=0:FORT%=1TOW%-1:IFZ$=W$(T%)FLAG=1
180 NEXTT%:IFFLAG=1GOTO155ELSEW$(W%)=Z$:NEXTW%
190 PROCFIT:MODE1:PROCDISPLAY:TIME=0:WIN=0
200
210 REM - Game loop ************
220
230 COLOUR3:*FX15,0
240 VDU28,0,31,39,26,12
250 INPUT"Word ",W$:IFW$="QUIT"GOTO450
260 INPUT"Row of initial letter ",R%
270 INPUT"Column of initial letter ",C%
280 PROCLCASE(W$)
290 WN%=1
300 IFY$=W$(WN%)GOTO330
310 WN%=WN%+1:IFWN%<=18GOTO300
320 PRINT"NOT IN THE PUZZLE":GOTO510
330 RESTORE:FORX%=1TOD%(WN%,3):READI%,J%:NEXT:X%=1
340 IFA$(C%,R%)<>MID$(Y$,X%,1)GOTO380
350 R%=R%+J%:C%=C%+I%
360 IFR%=0 OR R%=10 OR C%=20 OR C%=0 GOTO380
370 X%=X%+1:IFX%<=LEN(Y$)GOTO340ELSE390
380 PRINT"Word not in that position.":GOTO510
390 VDU26:COLOUR2:C%=D%(WN%,1):R%=D%(WN%,2)
400 FORX%=1TOLENY$:pRINTTAB(C%*2-1,R%*2-2);A$(C%,R%)
410 R%=R%+J%:C%=C%+I%:NEXT
420 PRINTTAB((WN%-1)MOD3*15,(WN%-1)DIV3+18);Y$
430 WIN=WIN+1:IFWIN<DONE GOTO230
440 X$="Finished at ":GOTO490
```

```
450 VDU26:COLOUR2
460 FORX%=1TO9:FORY%=1TO19
470 PRINT" ";:IF B$(Y%,X%)=""PRINT" ";ELSEPRINTB$(Y%,X%);
480 NEXT:COLOUR3:PRINT':NEXT:X$="Quit at "
490 VDU28,0,31,39,26,12
500 PRINT;X$;STR$(TIME/6000);" minutes.":END
510 INPUT"Press RETURN....",Q$:GOTO240
520
530 DEFPROCDBL(X%,Y%,C%,X$)
540 PRINTTAB(X%,Y%);CHR$141;CHR$C%;X$
550 PRINTTAB(X%,Y%+1);CHR$141;CHR$C%;X$:ENDPROC
560
570 DEFPROCWORDSIN
580 FORW%=1TO18:PRINT';"Word #";W%;
590 INPUTX$:IFLENX$>1OX$=LEFT$(X$,10)
600 PROCLCASE(X$):W$(W%)=Y$:NEXT
610 ENDPROC
620
630 DEFPROCFIT:DONE=0:FORW%=1TO18:TRY=0
640 TRY=TRY+1:IFTRY>"5W$(W%)="":GOTO750
650 X%=RND(18):Y%=RND(9):D%=RND(8):X1%=X%:Y1%=Y%
660 RESTORE:FORV%=1TOD%:READI%,J%:NEXT:L%=1
670 IFA$(X%,Y%)<>""ANDMID$(W$(W%),L%,1)<>A$(X%,Y%)GOTO640
680 X%=X%+I%:Y%=Y%+J%:IFX%=0ORX%=19ORY%=0ORY%=10GOTO640
690 L%=L%+1:IFL%<=LEN(W$(W%))GOTO670
700 D%(W%,1)=X1%:D%(W%,2)=Y1%:D%(W%,3)=D%:DONE=DONE+1
710 FORL%=1TOLEN(W$(W%))
720 A$(X1%,Y1%)=MID$(W$(W%),L%,1)
730 X1%=X1%+I%:Y1%=Y1%+J%
740 NEXT L%
750 NEXTW%
760 FORX%=1TO19:FORY%=1TO9
770 B$(X%,Y%)=A$(X%,Y%):NEXT:NEXT
780 FORX%=1TO19:FORY%=1TO9
790 IFA$(X%,Y%)=""THENA$(X%,Y%)=CHR$(RND(26)+96)
800 NEXT:NEXT:ENDPROC
810
820 DEFPROCDISPLAY
830 FORY%=1TO9:FORX%=1TO19
835 PROCLCASE(A$(X%,Y%))
840 PRINT" ";Y$;:NEXT
850 PRINT':NEXT:COLOUR1
860 PRINTCHR$11;L$;L$
870 FORX%=0TO5:FORY%=0TO2
880 PRINTTAB(Y%*15,X%+18);W$(X%*3+Y%+1)
890 NEXT:NEXT
900 PRINTTAB(0,24);L$;L$:COLOUR2:ENDPROC
910
920 DEFPROCLCASE(X$)
930 Y$="":FOR Z%=1 TO LENX$
940 IF ASC(MID$(X$,Z%,1))>=97 Y$=Y$+MID$(X$,Z%,1):GOTO960
950 Y$=Y$+CHR$(ASC(MID$(X$,Z%,1))+32)
960 NEXT:ENDPROC
970
```

```
 980 DATA1,-1,1,0,1,1,0,1,-1,1,-1,0,-1,-1,0,-1
 990 DATAcomputer,disk,screen,television,star,moon,book,volume
1000 DATAgirl,boy,father,mother,teacher,desk,school,pencil
1010 DATArubber,ruler,boxer,wrestler,terminal,backup,pear,apple
1020 DATAacorn,fruit,orange,banana,pomegranate,personal
1030 DATAspectacles,bed,chair,table,carpet,sideboard,bench
1040 DATAwindow,wall,door,ceiling,floor,kitchen,bathroom
1050 DATAbedroom,recorder,piano,flute,violin,accordion,|cello
1060 DATAtrumpet,drum,trombone,viola,garden,grass,trees
1070 DATAflower,petal,leaf,daisy,carnation,cooker,padlock
```

17

Derby

Another old favourite, especially when a group of friends congregate and shout themselves hoarse cheering on their fancied nag. Up to six can play, each starting with £100. The 'meet' starts at 2.00 pm and goes on until 6.00 pm, with a race every 15 minutes' game time, stopping sooner if any player runs out of cash. There is a pool of 20 horses, each with its own handicap. Only six horses are randomly selected out of the pool, so the possible permutations of horses running against each other are enormous. In addition, after every race the winning horse has its handicap increased – as per Jockey Club rules – while the others have theirs reduced. Similarly, Honest Joe the bookie will shorten the odds on winning horses and lengthen them on losers. The result is that it is a good test of judgement and skill at picking winners.

The first screen gives the title and asks for the number of players. The second screen seeks each player's name and then we move into the game loop, which consists of three more screens. The first is Honest Joe. We are given the number of six horses, their names and odds, and each player in turn is asked for his or her bet – the number of the horse backed and the amount.

The next screen is the race proper, and comprises four broad bands of green representing sections of the course. For verisimilitude we add posts and rails, a winning post and the start line, behind which we see the six horses and riders. As a reminder, the horses' names are opposite each. On pressing RETURN, the names disappear and the six horses race forward. As they reach the right edge of one section, they appear at the left edge of the one above, continuing in this way until one reaches the finish. The name of the winning horse is thrown on the screen and the action is frozen while players argue, if they feel like it – although it won't do them any good!

The final screen addresses each player by name and gives news of what happened to their bet and their current cash state. If all have cash the game time is advanced and we return to Honest Joe Bloggs to place bets for the next race.

Line 20 redefines a graphics character for horse and rider. The next lines prepare for coloured print, print the title and get the number of players, with line 140 DIMensioning the appropriate arrays. Line 200 prints requests to players in differentiating colours – a further aid to identification – and the next lines assign starting handicaps for each horse.

Line 320 prepares the next screen, with Joe Bloggs's billboard header. Lines 250 to 310 have picked the six horses running and ensured that there are no duplicates; now we have a printout. Player's bets are accepted and checked and on line 600 we start to print the course. This is done by redefining the graphics area and clearing it to background green four times before drawing the rails, etc., on top. It will be remembered that CHR$224 has been redefined as the horse-and-rider graphic symbol; it is seen that the horses are placed in position in line 710, with the next lines printing the name by the side of each. The fearsome lines 880, 900 and 920 do the calculations to ensure that the correct horse graphic is alternately rubbed out and redrawn in its new position. The idea to grasp here is that the calculations are based upon a totally linear course, progressing from value 0 to 4888, and that dividing its linear position by 1279 gives the displayed row or portion of the course.

Variables

D$	Start of line, yellow on blue
E$	Ditto, red on blue
F$	Spaces for clearance purposes
X%	General counter
PL%	Number of players
P%(PL%,2)	Players' cash and bets
P$(PL%)	Players' names
H%(20,2)	Horses' handicaps and odds (Pool)
R%(6,3)	Ditto (in current race), plus position
H$(20)	Horses' names
HR%	Game time; hour
MIN%	Game time; minutes
P%	Current player being addressed
Q$	Dummy
Y%	General counter

Z%	Ditto, used when checking against duplicates
W%	Ditto, used when getting wager
H%	Horse being bet on
T%	Position of current horse
W%	Number of winning horse
SP%	Odds (starting price) of winner

```
 10 REM - Derby
 20 VDU23,224,8,24,26,127,188,36,66,129
 30 MODE7:S$=STRING$(30," ")
 40 D$=CHR$132+CHR$157+CHR$131
 50 E$=CHR$132+CHR$157+CHR$129
 60 F$=STRING$(10," ")+STRING$(10,CHR$8)
 70 FORX%=5 TO 15 STEP 10
 80 PRINTTAB(0,X%);CHR$129;STRING$(19,"oO"):NEXT
 90 PROCDBL(12,9,137,"DERBY DAY")
100 REPEAT
110 PRINTTAB(0,17):"How many players (1-6)";:PL%=GET-48
120 PRINT;PL%
130 UNTIL PL%>0 AND PL%<7
140 DIM P%(PL%,2),P$(PL%),H%(20,2),R%(6,3),H$(20)
150 CLS:FORX%=1 TO 20:READ H$(X%):NEXT
160 HR%=2:MIN%=0
170 PRINT'''"Please input your names -"
180 FOR P%=1 TO PL%
200 PRINT'CHR$(P%MOD7+128);"Player #";P%;"...";
210 INPUT P$(P%):P%(P%,0)=100
220 NEXT:INPUT'''"Press RETURN...",Q$
230 FOR X%=1 TO 20
240 H%(X%,1)=RND(5)+3:H%(X%,2)=RND(3):NEXT
250 FOR X%=1 TO 6
260 Y%=RND(20)
270 FOR Z%=1 TO X%-1
280 IF Y%=R%(Z%,0) GOTO260 ELSE NEXT Z%
290 R%(X%,0)=Y%:R%(X%,1)=H%(Y%,1)
300 R%(X%,2)=H%(Y%,2):R%(X%,3)=0
310 NEXT X%
320 MODE7
330 PRINTD$'D$;
340 PRINT"H O N E S T    J O E   B L O G G S"
350 PRINTD$'E$'E$;
360 PRINT"******   M I C R O M E E T   ******"
370 PRINTE$
380 PRINTE$;" RUNNERS AND PRICES FOR  ";HR%;":";MIN%;" pm."
390 PRINTE$
400 FOR X%=6 TO 1 STEP -1
410 VDU130,157,132:PRINT"No.";R%(X%,0);
420 PRINTTAB(8);H$(R%(X%,0));TAB(27);R%(X%,1);" to 1"
430 NEXT
440 FOR W%=1 TO PL%
450 PRINTTAB(0,15):FOR X%=1 TO 8:PRINTS$:NEXT
460 REPEAT:PRINTTAB(0,15);P$(W%);" -"
```

```
 470 PRINT'"You have £";P%(W%,0)
 480 PRINT"How much do you bet";F$;
 490 INPUTP%(W%,1)
 500 UNTIL P%(W%,1)<=P%(W%,0) AND P%(W%,1)>0
 510 PRINTTAB(0,19);"On which number horse";F$;
 520 INPUT H%:X%=1
 530 IF R%(X%,0)=H% GOTO560
 540 X%=X%+1:IF X%<=6 GOTO530
 550 PRINT'"Horse #";H%;" not running.":GOTO510
 560 RESTORE:FORZ%=1TOH%:READH$:NEXT
 570 PRINT'"£";P%(W%,1);" on ";H$;" accepted."''
 580 INPUT"Press RETURN...",Q$
 590 P%(W%,2)=H%:NEXT W%
 600 REM - Prepare course
 610 MODE2:VDU18,0,130,16,18,0,132,0,0,0
 620 VDU24,0;232;1279;276;16,24,0;490;1279;534;16
 630 VDU24,0;748;1279;794;16,26,19,13,0,0,0,0
 640 REM - Finishing post and rails
 650 GCOL0,7:MOVE 1120,794:DRAW 1120,1023
 660 COLOUR1:COLOUR 130:PRINTTAB(17,0);"o"
 670 FORX%=232 TO 1002 STEP 258:PROCFENCE(X%):NEXT
 680 REM - Starting gate line-up
 690 MOVE 66,0:DRAW 66,232
 700 VDU5,18,4,0
 710 FOR X%=1 TO 6:MOVE 0,32*X%+32:PRINTCHR$224:NEXT:VDU4
 720 FOR X%=1TO6:RESTORE
 730 FOR Y%=1 TO R%(X%,0):READ H$:NEXT
 740 PRINTTAB(2,31-X%);H$:NEXT
 750 PRINTTAB(0,10);"UNDER ORDERS....";
 760 INPUT Q$:PRINTTAB(0,10);S$
 770 COLOUR2
 780 FOR X%=1TO6:RESTORE
 790 FOR Y%=1 TO R%(X%,0):READ H$:NEXT
 800 PRINTTAB(2,31-X%);H$*NEXT
 810 PRINTTAB(0,10);"THEY'RE OFF!"
 820 Q=INKEY(50):PRINTTAB(0,10);S$:VDU5:H%=0
 830
 840 REM - THE RACE *****************
 850
 860 REPEAT
 870 FOR X%=1 TO 6
 880 MOVE R%(X%,3)MOD1279,(R%(X%,3)DIV1279)*256+32*X%+32
 890 PRINTCHR$224
 900 T%=R%(X%,3)+R%(X%,2)+RND(20)+20
 910 R%(X%,3)=T%
 920 MOVE T%MOD1279,(T%DIV1279)*256+32*X%+32
 930 PRINTCHR$224
 940 IF T%>H% H%=T%
 950 NEXT:UNTIL H%>=4888
 960
 970 REM - Find & give winner
 980 W%=0:H%=0
 990 FORX%=1 TO 6:IF R%(X%,3)>H% H%=R%(X%,39:W%=R%(X%,0)
1000 NEXT X%:VDU4:COLOUR 9
```

```
1010 PRINTTAB(0,11);H$(W%);" wins!"TAB(0,17):SP%=H%(W%,1)
1020 COLOUR0:INPUTTAB(2,17),Q$:MODE7
1030
1040 REM - Tote - adjust cash
1050 FOR X%=1 TO PL%:CLS
1060 PROCDBL(5,5,131,P$(X%))
1070 PRINT''"Your £";P%(X%,1);
1080 PRINT" bet on #";P%(X%,2);" (";H$(P%(X%,2));")"''
1090 IF P%(X%,2)=W% GOTO1130
1100 PROCDBL(5,11,129,"LOST")
1110 P%(X%,0)=P%(X%,0)-P%(X%,1)
1120 GOTO1150
1130 PROCDBL(5,11,130,"WIN!"):PRINT''"At ";SP%;" to 1!"
1140 P%(X%,0)=P%(X%,0)+P%(X%,1)*SP%
1150 PRINT''"You have £";P%(X%,0)''''"Press RETURN....";
1160 INPUT G$:NEXT X%:CLS
1170 FOR X%=1 TO PL%:IF P%(X%,0)<=0 PROCEND:END
1180 NEXT
1190
1200 REM - Adjust race time
1210 MIN%=MIN%+15:IF MIN%=60 MIN%=0:HR%=HR%+1
1220 IF HR%>=6 PROCEND:END
1230 REM - Adjust prices & handicaps
1240 FOR X%=1 TO 6
1250 IF R%(X%,0)<>W% GOTO1290
1260 H%(R%(X%,0),1)=H%(R%(X%,0),1)-1
1270 H%(R%(X%,0),2)=H%(R%(X%,0),2)-1
1280 GOTO1310
1290 H%(R%(X%,0),1)=H%(R%(X%,0),1)+1
1300 H%(R%(X%,0),2)=H%(R%(X%,0),2)+1
1310 NEXT:GOTO250:REM - NEXT RACE
1320
1330 DEFPROCDBL(X%,Y%,C%,X$)
1340 PRINTTAB(X%,Y%);CHR$C%;CHR$141;X$
1350 PRINTTAB(X%,Y%+1);CHR$C%;CHR$141;X$
1360 ENDPROC
1370
1380 DEFPROCSPB
1390 PRINTTAB(0,23);"Press SPACEBAR to continue....";
1400 REPEAT:G$=GET$:UNTIL G$=" "
1410 ENDPROC
1420
1430 DATA Uncle Vanya,Running Wild,Spindrift,Owzyafarver
1440 DATA White Tornado,Speedy Gonzalez,Saucy Minx,Black Friar
1450 DATA Lively Lady,Spindleshanks
1460 DATA My Hope,Baker's Boy,Sweetheart,Fred's Fancy
1470 DATA Gillian Girl,Nosey Parker,Wild One,Muggins
1475 DATA Chipmunk,Silver Star
1480
1490 DEFPROCEND
1500 CLS:PROCDBL(2,2,131,"CASH AT END")
1510 PRINT':FORX%=1 TO PL%
1520 PRINTP$(X%);TAB(20);"£";P%(X%,0)
1530 NEXT:PRINT
```

```
1540 PROCDBL(0,31,129,"THAT'S ALL FOLKS!"):ENDPROC
1550
1560 DEFPROCFENCE(Y%)
1570 MOVE 0,Y%:DRAW 1279,Y%
1580 MOVE 0,Y%+40:DRAW 1279,Y%+40
1590 FOR S%=1 TO 1279 STEP 100
1600 MOVE S%,Y%:DRAW S%,Y%+40:NEXT
1610 ENDPROC
```

18

Bingo

It is no bad thing to make concessions to other members of the family, especially when one has hogged the TV for hours on end! Here is a computer implementation of Bingo that four can play and which should convince some members of the family that the computer can be of interest to all.

All players start with £10 and a 'card' costs £1, the winner being the one first to have a full card. The computer asks for the number of people playing and the time allowance. This latter is the time delay in seconds before the next number is called. To start with, allow about 7 or 8 seconds and decrease it as players become expert. The screen clears and then each player is asked to type in his or her name. When this is done, the screen again clears and a Bingo card is drawn for each player, each in his own colour, complete with number and name. Each card has twelve numbers and they are arranged as a normal Bingo card, lowest on the left, with values 11 to 99.

The game now starts. As the computer 'calls' each new number, players' attention is drawn by a short beep, and players must claim any that they have. That is to say, the computer will not automatically tag or cover the numbers on each card (that would be boring), but instead the player(s) must press a number 1, 2, 3 or 4, corresponding to their own player or card number. The computer will then cover the player's number – unless he or she is fibbing or mistaken – and restart the time delay. In this way, two or more players may claim the same called number. When the time allowance is up, with no player claiming, another number is called automatically. Note very carefully that if a player misses a claim, it is still possible that he or she can win, for in lines 220 to 240 the program makes 20 tries at finding an uncalled number before giving up and blanking the whole lot again. This provision is necessary because – at the faster auto speeds – it is conceivably possible that all players may miss at least one called number and therefore that no-one could win unless numbers were called again. There is no penalty for a wrong claim. The computer automatically checks for a winning card and adjusts cash accordingly before presenting a new set of Bingo cards.

The array C(X,Y) is the data concerning the players, with X the player's number and Y the 12 numbers on his or her card. After the usual input of names, PROCSHUFFLE blanks off the 'caller's' sheet, as it were, and then PROCARRAY creates and prints the player's card. It does this, starting at line 930, by first choosing 12 random numbers, ensuring that no two are alike, and then arranging them in ascending order (lines 1010 to 1050). The heading is printed by lines 1070 and 1080, and the three lines of the actual card are printed. For each row of data there are nine places to be printed or not, depending upon the next number; if when divided by ten it is greater than the current horizontal position, it is printed. Every third number is taken, with the starting bias depending upon the row number. For each horizontal position, therefore, either the number is printed, with padding spaces (lines 1120 and 1130), or else four graphics blocks are printed (line 1140). This is repeated as many times as necessary, being called by line 180 of the main program.

When RETURN is pressed, we enter the main game loop. The computer calls a number by choosing at random, checking that the N(X) array is blank (the number not having been called before). If it has been called, it makes another try and after 20 unsuccessful tries blanks the sheet off again. If all is well, the number is called, the VDU7 command causing a short beep.

The program now waits for a period of time set by the players, and if no input is detected on line 310, goes to choose another number to call. On an input, PL% is a legal player number, and the next lines check that the called number is on the player's card and not yet blanked off. Lines 380 to 400 calculate the position of the number on the screen and blank it by printing a small magenta marker over it. Line 410 actually blanks the number in the player's array.

Any successfully called number may result in a winning card, so now we check. If any element is found unblanked, that card is not yet full, so the game can proceed. Otherwise the screen is cleared, the winner announced and the cash adjusted. Pressing RETURN clears the screen for another set of cards.

Variables

P$(X)	Players' names
P(X)	Players' cash balances
C(X,Y)	Values on cards, where X = player and Y has 12 elements
N(X)	Caller's 'sheet', where 0 = uncalled number
G%	Number of players
TA%	Time allowance in seconds before another number is called
X%	General counter
X$	Transfer string from PROCbox
TRY%	Computer's tries at finding an uncalled number
N%	Current called number
PL%	Current player claiming a number
Y%	General counter
I%	Horizontal tab position for blanking piece on screen
J%	Vertical tab position for blanking piece on screen
Q%	Counter when checking for winning card

In PROCARRAY:

O%	Current number to be placed on card
N%	Count of numbers to be placed on card or checked
P%	Counter when checking for duplicates
FLAG%	Value = 1 when swap has taken place in sorting
Z%	Simple holding variable for swap process
R%	Number of row to be printed
C%	Character position in row

```
 10 MODE7:PROCTITLE("BINGO")
 20 DIM P$(4),P(4),C(4,12),N(99)
 30 PRINT''"How many players (1-4)?";
 40 REPEAT:G%=GET-48:UNTIL G%>0 AND G%<5:PRINT;G%
 50 INPUT'"Time allowance (1-9 secs)",TA%:TA%=TA%*100
 60 PRINT'"You all start with £10"
 70 PRINT'"Cards cost £1 each.":PROCRET
 80 CLS:PRINT''"Please type your names:"
 90 FOR X%=1 TO G%:P(X%)=10
100 PRINTTAB(0,X%*4);"Player #";X%
110 PROCbox(12,X%*4,12,1,148,0)
120 P$(X%)=X$:NEXT:PROCRET
130
140 REM - Outer loop
150
160 PROCSHUFFLE
```

```
170 CLS:FOR X%=1 TO G%
180 PROCARRAY(X%):NEXT:PROCRET
190
200 REM - Game loop
210
220 TRY%=1
230 N%=RND(89)+10:IF N(N%)=0 GOTO260
240 TRY%=TRY%+1:IF TRY%<=20 GOTO230
250 PROCSHUFFLE:GOTO220
260 N(N%)=N%:VDU7
270 VDU28,0,24,39,21,12
280 PRINTTAB(0,20);"Number called - ";N%
290 *FX15,1
300 PL%=INKEY(TA%)-48
310 IF PL%=-49 GOTO220
320 IF PL%<=0 OR PL%>G% GOTO300
330 Y%=1
340 IF C(PL%,Y%)=N% GOTO380
350 Y%=Y%+1:IF Y%<=12 GOTO340
360 PRINT;"Player ";PL%;" does not have ";N%;" on card."
370 PROCRET:GOTO270
380 I%=C(PL%,Y%)DIV10*4-3
390 J%=(PL%-1)*5+Y%MOD3:IFY%MOD3=0 J%=J%+3
400 VDU26:PRINTTAB(I%,J%);CHR$149;CHR$255;CHR$255
410c(PL%,Y%)=0
420
430 REM - Check for win
440
450 Q%=1
460 IF C(PL%,Q%)<>0 GOTO270
470 Q%=Q%+1:IF Q%<=12 GOTO460
480 VDU26:CLS:PROCDBL(0,3,131,P$(PL%)+" WINS")
490 FOR Y%=1 TO G%
500 IF PL%=Y% P(Y%)=P(Y%)+G%-1 ELSE P(Y%)=P(Y%)-1
510 NEXT Y%:PRINT"CASH -":FOR X%=1 TO G%
520 PRINT;P$(X%);" - £";P(X%):NEXT
530 PROCRET:GOTO160
540 DEFPROCTITLE(X$)
550 PRINTCHR$132;STRING$(19,"Oo")
560 PROCDBL((36-LEN(X$))/2,3,131,X$)
570 PRINT'CHR$132;STRING$(19,"Oo")
580 ENDPROC
590
600 DEFPROCDBL(X%,Y%,C%,X$)
610 PRINTTAB(X%,Y%);CHR$141;CHR$C%;X$
620 PRINTTAB(X%,Y%+1);CHR$141;CHR$C%;X$
630 ENDPROC
640
650 DEFPROCbox(X%,Y%,L%,H%,C%,F%)
660 LOCALV%,W%,I%,J%:REM - MODE7 ONLY
670 PRINTTAB(X%,Y%);
680 V%=VPOS:W%=POS:PRINTTAB(W%,V%-H%);CHR$C%;"7";
690 FORI%=0TOL%+1:PRINT"£";:NEXT:PRINT"k"
700 PRINTTAB(W%,V%+1);CHR$C%;"u";
```

```
 710 FORI%=0TOL%+1:PRINT"p";:NEXT:PRINT"z"
 720 FORJ%=V%-H%+1TOV%:PRINTTAB(W%,J%);CHR$C%;"5":NEXT
 730 FORJ%=V%-H%+1TOV%
 740 PRINTTAB(W%+L%+3,J%);CHR$C%;"j":NEXT
 750 IF F%GOTO860
 760 PRINTTAB(W%+2,V%);CHR$135;
 770 FORI%=1TOL%:PRINT".";:NEXT
 780 PRINTTAB(W%+3,V%);:X$=""
 790 G$=GET$:IF ASCG$=13 GOTO860
 800 IF LENX$=L%OR ASCG$=127 GOTO820
 810 PRINT G$;:X$=X$+G$:GOTO790
 820 IF X$="" GOTO790
 830 X$=LEFT$(X$,LENX$-1):PRINTCHR$8;
 840 IF ASCG$<>127 GOTO810
 850 PRINT".";CHR$8;:GOTO790
 860 ENDPROC
 870
 880 DEFPROCRET
 890 PRINTTAB(5,24);CHR$131;"Press";
 900 PRINTCHR$132;CHR$157;CHR$129;"RETURN ";CHR$156;
 910 G$=GET$:ENDPROC
 920
 930 DEFPROCARRAY(X%)
 940 LOCAL N%,O%,P%,Z%,FLAG%
 950 FOR N%=1 TO 12
 960 O%=RND(89)+10:P%=1
 970 IF C(X%,P%)=O% GOTO960
 980 P%=P%+1:IF P%<N% GOTO970
 990 C(X%,N%)=O%:NEXT
1000 REM - Arrange in order
1010 FLAG%=0:FOR N%=1 TO 11
1020 IF C(X%,N%)<=C(X%,N%+1)GOTO1050
1030 Z%=C(X%,N%):C(X%,N%)=C(X%,N%+1)
1040 C(X%,N%+1)=Z%:FLAG%=1
1050 NEXT N%:IF FLAG%<>0 GOTO1010
1060 REM - Print card
1070 PRINTCHR$150;CHR$157;CHR$132;
1080 PRINT;"PLAYER ";X%;" - ";P$(X%)
1090 FOR R%=1 TO 3:N%=R%:PRINTCHR$(144+X%);
1100 FOR C%=1 TO 9:IF N%>12 GOTO1140
1110 IF C(X%,N%)DIV10>C% GOTO1140
1120 PRINTCHR$135;:IFC(X%,N%)<10 PRINT" ";
1130 PRINT;C(X%,N%);CHR$(144+X%);:N%=N%+3:GOTO1150
1140 PRINTCHR$255;CHR$255;CHR$255;
1150 NEXT:PRINT:NEXT:PRINT
1160 ENDPROC
1170 DEFPROCSHUFFLE
1180 FOR X%=11 TO 99:N(X%)=0:NEXT
1190 ENDPROC
```

19

Anagram

In this version of the well-known puzzle, you may play against another person or against the computer. When two people play, one averts his head while the other types in a word for the computer to jumble up. When you play against the computer, a word is selected from those held in memory. Scores are maintained by counting the number of tries before the original word is recovered. Two players will arrange their own rules, but when playing against the computer, you may type Q for Quit, when the program will tell you what the word was and penalise you four points. One point is subtracted for each false try, but if you get the word, you gain one. Alter these values if you wish.

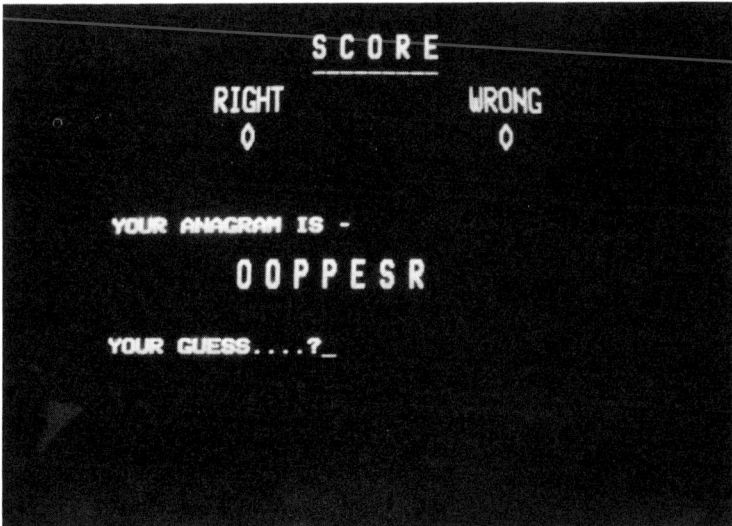

```
              S C O R E
        RIGHT              WRONG
          0                  0


  YOUR ANAGRAM IS -
        O O P P E S R

  YOUR GUESS....?_
```

The program naturally falls into two portions dealing with solo or two-player games, the split taking place on line 80. From there down to line 470 deals with the two-player version. Each player is asked for his or her name and then the first player is asked to type in a word (line 220). This should be at least five letters long, as set by line 230. PROCJUMBLE then muddles up the word. This is done very simply by having a parallel array called A%(X%), initially blank, and we 'cross off' or enter the value 1 when the corresponding letter of the word has been used. We choose a letter at random in line 910 and ensure that it has not been used. If OK, we add that letter to a growing muddled string, V$, in line 920. When all letters have been used – as evidenced by a simple count – we end the procedure. It will be seen that V$ is also padded out with spaces between the letters; this is for print purposes, making the anagram easier to read. The anagram is now held in V$ and the original word is still contained in W$·

Players are now switched by line 300. The second player is addressed and the anagram presented, printed double height for clarity. The player's guess is now accepted on line 320. If correct, a jump is made to line 370; if not, his score of errors is incremented and the display brought up to date by PROCSCORE. If preferred, another call to PROCJUMBLE on line 360 would jumble the word afresh before the user has another try.

When the word is successfully identified, a message is given and the two players change roles. Play proceeds in this way for ten rounds, the winner being the one with the lowest score.

When playing against the computer, the player is asked for a difficulty level or word length, from 4 letters to 12 – extend this if you like. There are ten rounds as before, but to ensure that the same word is not presented twice, the computer keeps a record of the word number in the array W%(X). The words are in groups of ten in lines 940 onwards, with ten four-letter words followed by ten five-letter, ten six-letter, and so on. If you like, you could increase the number of words – there must be the same number in each group – and alter the bracketed value in line 640, where the position of the word is chosen. The actual word itself is found and read in line 650, being transferred to W$, as required by PROC-JUMBLE, so if you change the number of words you will also have to change the '10' in line 650. The rest of the program is quite straightforward.

Variables

P$(2)	Names of players
P%(2)	Scores

A%(24)   Array for check when jumbling. 24 characters allowed!
W%(10)   Record of words (numbers) used
C$ A clearing string, printed to clear part of screen
SCORE%   Record of incorrect replies
R%   Record of correct replies
G$ General input string
X%   General counter
P%   Current player addressed or current problem (in solo game)
W$ Word input, or to be jumbled
Q$ Player's guess at anagram
G   Timing dummy
ROUNDS%   Record of rounds between players
WL%   Chosen word length

```
 10 REM - Anagram
 20 MODE7:DIM P$(2),P%(2),A%(24),W%(10)
 30 C$=STRING$(30," "):SCORE%=0:R%=0
 40 PROCDBL(9,5,129,"ANAGRAMS")
 50 PRINT'''"TYPE 'C' TO PLAY AGAINST THE COMPUTER"
 60 PRINT"OR 'P' TO PLAY AGAINST ANOTHER PERSON."'
 70 REPEAT:INPUT G$:UNTIL G$="C" OR G$="P"
 80 ROUNDS%=0:IF G$="C" GOTO600
 90 CLS:PRINT'''"PLEASE TYPE YOUR FIRST NAMES..."
100 FOR X%=1 TO 2:PRINT'''"PLAYER #";X%;"...."
110 INPUT P$(X%):NEXT:P%=1
120 CLS:PROCDBL(0,1,129,P$(1))
130 PROCDBL(20,1,129,P$(2))
140 PRINTTAB(0,3);CHR$129;" ";
150 PRINTSTRING$(LEN(P$(1)),"_");
160 PRINTTAB(22);STRING$(LEN(P$(2)),"_")
170
180 REM - GAME LOOP
190
200 PROCSCORE
210 PRINTTAB(0,12);P$(P%);" "'''
220 PRINT"PLEASE TYPE YOUR WORD"'':INPUT W$
230 IF LEN(W$)>4 GOTO250
240 PRINT"SOMETHING LONGER, PLEASE.":G$=GET$:GOTO120
250 PROCJUMBLE
260
270 REM - CLEAR SCREEN, PRESENT ANAGRAM
280
290 PRINTTAB(0,12);C$;TAB(0,14);C$;TAB(0,18);C$
300 P%=3-P%:PRINTTAB(0,7);P$(P%);" "
310 PRINT"YOUR ANAGRAM IS";PROCDBL(2,10,131,V$)
320 PRINTTAB(0,15);C$;CHR$13;:INPUT"YOUR WORD....",Q$
330 IF Q$=W$ GOTO370
```

```
340 P%(P%)=P%(P%)+1:PRINTTAB(0,18);"TRY AGAIN"
350 G=INKEY(100):PRINTTAB(0,18);C$
360 PROCSCORE:GOTO320
370 PROCDBL(6,18,134,"RIGHT!"):ROUNDS%=ROUNDS%+1
380 IF ROUNDS%>10 GOTO450
390 PRINT'"NOW YOU CHANGE OVER..."
400 PRINT"PRESS RETURN WHEN READY......";:G$=GET$
410 FOR X%=1 TO 24:A%(X%)=0:NEXT:GOTO120
420
430 REM - END OF CONTEST *********
440
450 CLS:PROCDBL(5,6,129,"FINAL SCORES")
460 FORX%=1 TO 2:PRINT''P$(X%);TAB(20);P%(X%):NEXT
470 END
480
490 DEFPROCDBL(X%,Y%,C%,X$)
500 PRINTTAB(X%,Y%);CHR$C%;CHR$141;X$
510 PRINTTAB(X%,Y%+1);CHR$C%;CHR$141;X$
520 ENDPROC
530
540 DEFPROCSCORE
550 PROCDBL(2,4,129,STR$(P%(1)))
560 PROCDBL(22,4,129,STR$(P%(2))):ENDPROC
570
580 REM - PLAY AGAINST COMPUTER
590
600INPUT'"WHAT WORD LENGTH (4-12)",WL%
610IF WL%<4 OR WL%>12 GOTO600 ELSE WL%=WL%-4
620 FOR X=1 TO 10:W%(X)=0:NEXT
630 FOR P%=1 TO 10:REM -TEN PROBLEMS
640 X%=RND(10):IF W%(X%)<>0 GOTO640 ELSE W%(X%)=99
650 RESTORE:FOR Y%=1 TO X%+10*WL%:READ W$:NEXT
660 CLS:PROCDBL(12,1,131,"S C O R E")
670 PRINTTAB(13);CHR$131;"            "
680 PROCDBL(5,4,130,"RIGHT"):PROCDBL(23,4,129,"WRONG")
690 PROCJUMBLE:PROCDBL(7,6,130,STR$(R%))
700 PROCDBL(25,6,129,STR$(SCORE%))
710 PRINTTAB(0,11);"YOUR ANAGRAM IS -"
720 PROCDBL(7,13,131,V$)
730FORX=1TO9:PRINTSTRING$(30," "):NEXT
740 PRINTTAB(0,17);"YOUR GUESS....";:INPUT Q$
750 IF Q$=W$ GOTO810 ELSE SCORE%=SCORE%+1
760 IF Q$<>"Q" GOTO800
770 PRINT'CHR$131;"THE ANSWER IS"
780 PROCDBL(14,19,129,CHR$136+W$)
790 G=INKEY(1000):SCORE%=SCORE%+4:GOTO830
800 PRINT''"TRY AGAIN....":GOTO690
810 VDU7:PROCDBL(13,19,130,CHR$136+"RIGHT!"):R%=R%+1
820 PRINT'"PRESS RETURN WHEN READY...";:G$=GET$
830 NEXT P%:CLS:PRINTTAB(0,5):
840 PRINT"YOUR SCORE WAS ";R%;" OUT OF 10"'
850 INPUT"PLAY AGAIN (Y-N)",Q$:IF Q$<>"N"R%=0:GOTO600
860 END
870
```

```
880 DEFPROCJUMBLE
890 FOR X%=1 TO 20:A%(X%)=0:NEXT
900 V$="":X$="":FOR X%=1 TO LEN(W$)
910 Y%=RND(LEN(W$)):IF A%(Y%)<>0 GOTO910
920 A%(Y%)=1:V$=V$+MID$(W$,Y%,1)+" "
930 NEXT:ENDPROC
935
940 DATAGODS,FOAM,PIPE,LADY,ZOOM,CANE,DESK,BOOK,CELL,CHIP
950 DATAMESSY,GLOVE,CHESS,CIGAR,GLASS,CHUTE,BOOTS,MATCH
960 DATAGHOST,LOCKS,DONKEY,CONTENT,VOLUME,BIGGER,SADDLE
965 DATAREPEAT,CHANGE,CRUNCH,HAMMER,CITIES,CHIMNEY,DRAWING
970 DATAMANHUNT,TOBACCO,CABINET,SCARLET,COMMAND,PROPOSE
975 DATACURTAIN,CHESTNUT,MINISTER,LIFEBELT,COMPUTER,IDENTITY
980 DATATELETEXT,CHASTISE,FILIGREE,PARAPETS,RUNABOUT
990 DATAINFLATED,ELONGATED,REDUCTION,VANISHING,CARNATION
998 DATAJACOBITES,JUDGEMENT,PARTITION,STROLLING,SWINEHERD
999 DATAACCOMPANY,FAVOURABLE,UNDEFENDED,OPERATIONS
1000 DATAEVENTUALLY,REPUTATION,CHANDELIER,LOCOMOTIVE
1005 DATASEAMANSHIP,ZOOLOGICAL,WRISTBANDS,PROGRESSION
1010 DATABENEVOLENCE,MATERIALIZE,WEIGHBRIDGE,CONSOLIDATE
1015 DATADELINQUENTS,REGURGITATE,TEMPESTUOUS,ASSASSINATE
1020 DATAAGRICULTURE,INCINERATORS,EXTINGUISHER,ABSTRACTIONS
1030 DATASURVEILLANCE,DISENCHANTED,MISCALCULATE,UNQUESTIONED
1040 DATAACQUAINTANCE,RELINQUISHED,OBSTRUCTIONS
```

20

Simon

A simple game, this; a computer implementation of the well-known game. The computer flashes a sequence of coloured squares, each accompanied by its own note, and the user attempts to duplicate it. As he does so, the same coloured squares flash and the same notes are emitted. The program starts by asking for a difficulty level, which determines the length of time each square is displayed, then begins the sequence with only one item. If successful, the sequence is lengthened by one each time and this continues until the player makes an error.

The listing is quite interesting. The VDU19 commands turn all colours to black and then the four calls to PROCSQ draw (invisibly) the four squares, each in a different computer colour. Similarly, for speed the message 'READY!' and the prompt '. . . . . . ?' are preprinted on the screen invisibly. Adopting this method, all that we need do is change appropriate computer colours (confusing, that; all colours are black at this point!) to their real or screen colours for them to appear immediately. In line 220, for example, changing logical colour 15 makes the message 'READY!' appear. Line 230 times it for three seconds, and then line 240 switches it off again. Simple!

The variable called GO% specifies the overall length of the series so far correctly remembered and stored in A%(X), and the variable SEG% is the current one. The appropriate colour is switched in line 290, with accompanying sound in line 300. This makes the square appear, before it is switched off again in line 320 after a period of time determined by D%· Line 340 switches another colour, causing the prompt '. . . . . . ?' to appear, which is the signal for the player to repeat the sequence he or she has just seen.

Player input is at line 360. He is required to press R, G, B or Y (for red, green, blue and yellow), as appropriate. No RETURN is necessary. If correct, line 430 switches the proper colour and sounds the note. The colour is switched back again by line 450.

Variables

A%(30)	Array to hold each item of the series, up to 30
D%	Difficulty level
GO%	Length of series so far
G$	Dummy
SEG%	Current item of the series
C%	Colour to be switched
Q%	Count of user's inputs
Q$	User's input; R, G, B or Y
NOW	Timer for display

```
   5 REM - Simon
  10 MODE7:DIM A%(30)
  20 PROCDBL(12,5,"SIMON")
  30 PRINTTAB(13,7);CHR$130;"      "''
  40 PRINT''''"How difficult?"''
  50 PRINT"Type a number from 1 (hard) to 9 (easy)"''
  60 REPEAT:D%=INKEY(0):UNTIL D%>48 AND D%<58:D%=D%-48
  70 MODE2
  80
  90 REM - Print squares in black
 100
 110 VDU19,1,0,0,0,0,19,2,0,0,0,0,19,3,0,0,0,0
 120 VDU19,4,0,0,0,0,19,5,0,0,0,0,19,15,0,0,0,0,5
 130 PROCSQ(100,100,1):PROCSQ(600,100,2)
 140 PROCSQ(100,550,3):PROCSQ(600,550,4)
 150 MOVE 40,50:GCOL0,15:PRINT"READY!"
 160 MOVE 500,50:GCOL0,5:PRINT "......?"
 170
 180 REM - GAME LOOP *************
 190
 200 GO%=0
 210 REPEAT:GO%=GO%+1
 220 VDU19,15,15,0,0,0
 230 G$=INKEY$(300)
 240 VDU19,15,0,0,0,0
 250 A%(GO%)=RND(4)
 260 IF A%(GO%)=A%(GO%-1) GOTO250
 270 FOR SEG%=1 TO GO%
 280 C%=A%(SEG%)
 290 VDU19,C%,C%,0,0,0
 300 SOUND1,-10,C%*50,3
 310 TIME=0:REPEAT UNTIL TIME>=D%*20
 320 VDU19,C%,0,0,0,0
```

```
330 NEXT SEG%
340 VDU19,5,5,0,0,0:*FX15,0
350 FOR Q%=1 TO GO%
360 REPEAT:Q$=GET$
370 UNTIL Q$="R" OR Q$="Y" OR Q$="B" OR Q$="G"
380 IF Q$="R" AND A%(Q%)=1 GOTO430
390 IF Q$="G" AND A%(Q%)=2 GOTO430
400 IF Q$="Y" AND A%(Q%)=3 GOTO430
410 IF Q$="B" AND A%(Q%)=4 GOTO430
420 GOTO480
430 VDU19,A%(Q%),A%(Q%),0,0,0:SOUND1,-10,A%(Q%)*50,3
440 NOW=TIME
450 REPEAT UNTIL TIME>=NOW+25:VDU19,A%(Q%),0,0,0,0:NEXT
460 VDU19,5,0,0,0,0:REM - VANISH PROMPT
470 UNTIL 0
480 MODE7:VDU4:COLOUR 6
490 PRINTTAB(0,5);"YOU SCORED ";GO%-1
500 PRINT'''"TYPE RUN TO PLAY AGAIN."
510 END
520
530 DEFPROCDBL(X%,Y%,X$)
540 PRINTTAB(X%,Y%);:VDU 130,141:PRINT X$
550 PRINTTAB(X%,Y%+1);:VDU 130,141:PRINT X$
560 ENDPROC
570
580 DEFPROCSQ(X%,Y%,C%)
590 GCOL0,C%
600 MOVEX%,Y%:MOVEX%+500,Y%
610 PLOT81,-500,450
620 PLOT81,500,0
630 ENDPROC
```

21

Readnum

Here is a program that will give your kids practice in reading and understanding numbers, for it asks in English for a digital equivalent. For example, 'Type seven thousand three hundred and fifty eight'. The user is then expected to type 7358. The program will handle any number of digits from one to nine, so that young children can start to handle problems like, 'Type three', while older children will have things like, 'Type seventy seven million, three hundred and four thousand, nine hundred and twenty'.

If the input is incorrect, help is at hand, for the program will say, 'I asked you for eighty seven. You typed 800 – eight hundred'. In this way, the number values are constantly reinforced and results are guaranteed.

```
         I asked you for
         five thousand
         five hundred & ninety seven .


         You typed 5000
         five thousand




     Press RETURN to try again...
  ?_
```

The program is written around the subroutine starting at line 380. It is recursive, which is to say that it constantly calls itself as a subroutine. This definition immediately brings to mind two questions: (a) how do you get out of it, and (b) what is the purpose?

The first is no great trouble. One simply counts the number of recursive calls and ensures that there are the same number of RETURN commands encountered. The purpose of a recursive routine is to save programming space when the same operations or sequence of operations are to be performed repeatedly on data.

When we look at a set of digits such as 12345 and translate it as 'twelve thousand, three hundred and forty five', we have scanned the set of digits with the eye, starting from the *right*, and broken it down into groups of three. Each group of three has a name — thousands, millions — and within the group the digits are again given names such as hundreds, tens and units. The highest pair of digits that can be expressed as a single word — twelve, fifteen, or twenty — is detected, and as a postscript we add the name of the group.

To do the job, a computer program must follow the same rules, and since the operations performed on each group are the same, the program becomes recursive.

'Readnum' was first developed when a parent expressed concern that her child could not read numbers. It was altered slightly for *26 Programs for Your Micro* (Newnes Technical Books, 1982), and is here altered again to take advantage of the colour and double-size print offered by the BBC computer. It will find a variety of uses in the educational field, but even if you never use the program, it is worth 'hand-running' simply in order to get a feel for what a recursive program is and how it operates.

The bulk of the program listing is either straightforward or, in the case of the procedures, described elsewhere in this book, so we can move straight to a consideration of the subroutine.

Let us take for our example the value given — 12345. (You can try other, larger, numbers for yourself.) On entry into the routine at line 380, N contains our value 12345. At line 400 we are routed to line 500, where S is given the value 12345 and N is reduced to 12. This is our new N and the subroutine calls itself again, so we start back at 380.

This time, we pass line 400 and at 410 are routed to line 620. The READ pointer is restored to the beginning of the data (at line 770) by the RESTORE statement of line 620, and then we are routed to line 690. Lines 640 and 650 cause 'twelve' to be written into A$, and then calls to PROCS and PROCD cause the word 'twelve' to be printed on the screen. Going back to line 660, a RETURN statement is encountered. Unreeling itself, BASIC will find that its last GOSUB command was encountered at line 510, so command returns to the line following, at 520, which causes a printout of the word 'thousand'.

At line 540, N is given a new value by picking up the old value from the variable S and removing the thousands value. We are left with 345, and line 570 causes the process to repeat.

Again I recommend hand-running the program, using different numbers. The experience will teach you more about recursive subroutines than will a million words of text.

Variables

D%	Digits in the problem
PR%	Number of current problem
N%	Value chosen for current problem
N1	Copy of above
A$	General print string
TR%	User's tries
V	Numeric value of user's input
Q$	Dummy
N$	User's input as a string
B	Billions held over
M	Millions held over
S	Thousands held over
H	Hundreds held over

```
 10 REM - Readnum
 20 MODE7
 30 PROCDBL(5,5,131,"READING NUMBERS")
 40 PRINTTAB(6);CHR$131;"_____"
 50 PRINT"How many digits should the highest"
 60 PRINT"number have? (6 digits = 999999 maximum,"
 70 PRINT"but the program will handle any number"
 80 PRINT"of digits from 1 to 9.)"
 90 REPEAT:INPUT'"Your choice",D%:UNTIL D%>=1 AND D%<=9
100 REPEAT:INPUT'"How many problems",PROB%:UNTIL PROB%>=1
110
120 REM - Game loop
130
140 TR%=0:FOR PR%=1 TO PROB%
150 CLS:N=RND(10↑D%)-1:N1=N
160 PRINT'CHR$133;"Problem ";PR%
170 PROCDBL(0,3,131,"Type the number -"):PRINT:A$=""
180 TR%=TR%+1:IF D%=1 AND N=0 PROCS("nought"):GOTO200
190 GOSUB380
```

```
200 PROCS("."):PRINTTAB(12,15);:PROCBOX(D%,4)
210 IF V<>N1 GOTO250
220 PROCP:PROCDBL(13,18,129,CHR$136+A$)
230 PROCWARBLE:PROCDBL(12,22,130,"Press RETURN...")
240 INPUT Q$:GOTO310
250 CLS:PROCDBL(0,1,133,"I asked you for")
260 N=N1:GOSUB380:PROCS(".")
270 PROCDBL(0,11,133,"You typed "+N$)
280 N=V:GOSUB380
290 PROCDBL(0,22,129,"Press RETURN to try again...")
300 INPUT Q$:CLS:N=N1:GOTO160
310 NEXT PR%
320 CLS:PROCDBL(5,7,131,"The End")
330 PRINT''''"You did the"''PR%-1;" problems in ";TR%;" tries."
340 END
350
360 REM - Print numbers in English
370
380 IF N>1E9 GOTO420
390 IF N>1E6 GOTO440
400 IF N>1E3 GOTO500
410 IF N>99 GOTO560 ELSE GOTO620
420 B=N:N=INT(N/1E9):GOSUB380:PROCS("billion")
430 N=B-INT(B/1E9)*1E9:IF N=0 RETURN ELSE PRINT:PRINT
440 M=N:N=INT(N/1E6)
450 GOSUB380
460 PROCS("million")
470 N=M-INT(M/1E6)*1E6
480 IF N=0 RETURN
490 PRINT:PRINT
500 S=N:N=INT(N/1E3)
510 GOSUB380
520 PROCS("thousand")
530 PRINT:PRINT
540 N=S-INT(S/1000)*1000
550 IF N=0 RETURN
560 H=N:N=INT(N/100)
570 GOSUB620
580 PROCS("hundred")
590 N=H-INT(H/100)*100
600 IF N=0 RETURN
610 PROCS(" & ")
620 RESTORE
630 IF N>15 GOTO690
640 FOR D=1 TO N+1
650 READ A$:NEXT D
660 A$=A$+" ":PROCS(A$):IF N<21 RETURN
670 N=INT(N/10)*10
680 IF N=0 RETURN ELSE GOTO620
690 IF N>19 GOTO730
700 FOR D=1 TO N-9:READ A$:NEXT D
710 IF N=18 A$="eighteen":GOTO660
720 A$=A$+"teen":GOTO660
730 FOR D=1 TO INT(N/10)+15:READ A$:NEXT
```

```
 740 A$=A$+" ":PROCS(A$):N=N-INT(N/10)*10
 750 IF N=0 RETURN ELSE GOTO620
 760
 770 DATA no,one,two,three,four,five,six,seven,eight,nine
 780 DATA ten,eleven,twelve,thirteen,fourteen,fifteen
 790 DATA twenty,thirty,forty,fifty,sixty
 800 DATA seventy,eighty,ninety
 810
 820 DEFPROCDBL(X%,Y%,C%,X$)
 830 PRINTTAB(X%,Y%);CHR$141;CHR$C%;X$
 840 PRINTTAB(X%,Y%+1);CHR$141;CHR$C%;X$:ENDPROC
 850
 860 DEFPROCS(X$)
 870 PROCD(POS,VPOS)
 880 PRINTCHR$(11);
 890 ENDPROC
 900
 910 DEFPROCD(X%,Y%)
 920 IF X%>3 GOTO960
 930 PRINTTAB(0,Y%);CHR$141;CHR$131
 940 PRINTTAB(0,Y%+1);CHR$141;CHR$131
 950 X%=X%+2
 960 PRINTTAB(X%,Y%);X$
 970 PRINTTAB(X%,Y%+1);X$;
 980 ENDPROC
 990
1000 DEFPROCBOX(L%,C%)
1010 V%=VPOS:W%=POS
1020 PRINTTAB(W%,V%-1);CHR$(C%+144);"7";
1030 FOR I%=0 TO L%+1:PRINT"£";:NEXT:PRINT"k"
1040 PRINTTAB(W%,V%+1);CHR$(C%+144);"u";
1045 FOR I%=0 TO L%+1:PRINT"p";:NEXT:PRINT"z"
1050 PRINTTAB(W%,V%);CHR$(C%+144);"5"
1060 PRINTTAB(W%+L%+3,V%);CHR$(C%+144);"j"
1070 PRINTTAB(W%+2,V%);CHR$135;
1080 FORZ%=1TOD%:PRINT".";:NEXT
1090 PRINTTAB(W%+3,V%);:N$=""
1100 G$=GET$:IF ASC(G$)=13 THEN 1130
1110 IF LEN(N$)>=D% THEN N$=LEFT$(N$,D%-1):PRINTCHR$8;
1120 PRINTG$;:N$=N$+G$:GOTO1100
1130 V=VAL(N$):ENDPROC
1140
1150 DEFPROCWARBLE
1160 FORS%=1TO20:SOUND1,-12,30,1
1170 SOUND1,-12,100,1:NEXT:ENDPROC
1180
1190 DEFPROCP
1200 ON RND(6) GOTO1210,1220,1230,1240,1250,1260
1210 A$="Right!":ENDPROC
1220 A$="Hooray!":ENDPROC
1230 A$="Clever old you!":ENDPROC
1240 A$="Great!":ENDPROC
1250 A$="Smashing!":ENDPROC
1260 A$="How about that!":ENDPROC
```

22

Snap

In this game of Snap, the computer displays a word or numeric value left and right alternately – 'playing', as it were, both hands. To win the point, the user must tap a key within the time limit set by the difficulty level. If a key is pressed when the two sides do not match, or if the user is too late pressing a key, a point is lost. The scoring is rather different from usual. Both the computer and the player start with ten points and points are exchanged, one side increasing as the other decreases. The game ends when either side reaches twenty, the other side than having nil. As an added interest, the scores on both sides are shown numerically, and underneath is a bar-graph or column representing the score graphically.

The user has a choice of subject matter, given in lines 120 to 140 of the listing. These are alphabetic or numeric. If for example the

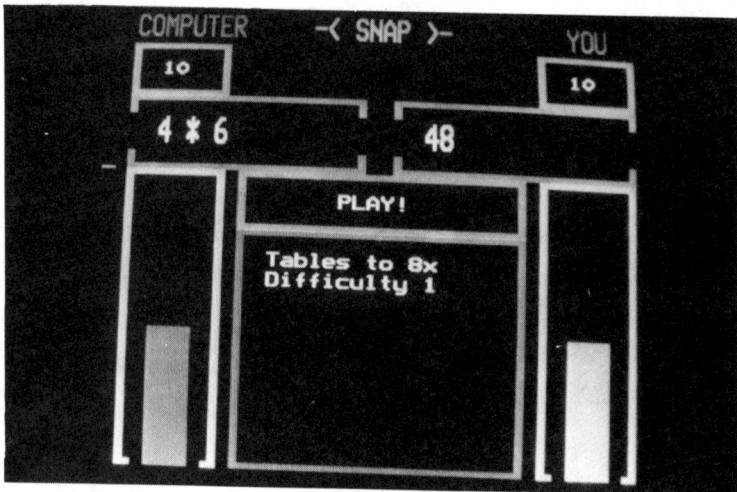

user chooses three-letter words, then a match is simple; the word on each side must be identical for the Snap point to be won. On the other hand, if a numeric subject is chosen it is the total value on each side that must match. That is to say, if one side displays 12, then the other side might show 3 + 9, or 4 * 3, for a Snap. As an improvement, readers might like to devise simple graphics, but as the program is written in Mode 7 we cannot utilise user-defined graphics or drawn pictures of any kind. On the other hand, there might be scope for a few letters printed in a variety of colours on different backgrounds.

As will be seen from the illustration PROCBOX is used a lot in this game, which helps to concentrate attention. The screen is cleared in line 20 and then down to line 150 we are concerned with preparing the display. The DATA lines pertain to information regarding the position, size and colour of the various boxes. Although you may not understand how it works, the listing down to line 390 should be easy enough to follow.

PROCGRAPH is responsible for printing the left and right bar-graphs, while PROCCLR clears the centre text box. When we reach the game loop, the user is warned with a flashing prompt (line 430) and then abruptly the word 'PLAY!' appears. The computer immediately starts playing characters into the left and right play areas.

PROCCHECK checks for a user input – Snap claim – and also checks to see if the two displays are the same. The scores and graphs are adjusted if necessary, as are the graphic displays.

Of all the listing, PROCCHOICE is the most interesting, as this is the procedure that prepares what is to appear in the two play areas. There is no problem if a choice of words was made, as line 1190 simply adjusts the READ pointer to the appropriate DATA line 1080 to 1120, but numeric values are entirely different and must be recalculated on every appearance. If you glance back at the user's original choices, you will see that in the numeric selection there are numbers to 10 (total), numbers to 20, tables to 4 times, tables to 8 times and tables to 12 times. Line 1200 splits the tables away from the others and in each case there is a 50 per cent chance that either the program will print a complete equation as in '4 + 9', or print the value as in '13'. Follow this part of the listing carefully and you will see the point. Remember that in BBC BASIC, the EVAL command causes the evaluation of the numeric parts of a string.

Variables

GR$	A short block-graphic string for the graphs
X	General counter
B$ and C$	Strings of spaces for clearance purposes

A%	Horizontal position of box
B%	Vertical position of box
C%	Length of box
D%	Height of box
E%	Colour of box
L%	Number of left play display
R%	Ditto, right
L1%, R1%	Copies of above
PS%	Player's score
CS%	Computer's score
Q$	Player's choice input
CH%	ASCII value of Q$
D	Difficulty level
K	Dummy; also used for Snap input
Z$	Numeric string to be evaluated or printed
Z%	Value of Z$

```
 10 REM - Snap
 20 MODE7:PROCDBL(0,0,129,"COMPUTER")
 30 GR$=CHR$255+CHR$255+CHR$255+CHR$149
 40 PROCDBL(31,0,129,"YOU")
 50 PROCDBL(13,0,131,"_< SNAP >_")
 60 FORX=1TO8
 70 READA%,B%,C%,D%,E%:PROCbox(A%,B%,C%,D%,E%):NEXT
 80 B$=STRING$(8," "):C$=B$+B$:L%=0:R%=0:L1%=0:R1%=0
 90 FORX=1TO2:PRINTTAB(0,5+X);C$;C$;B$:NEXT
100 DATA1,3,3,1,4,30,3,3,1,4,1,7,13,2,2,20,7,13,2
110 DATA2,9,10,16,1,4,1,22,3,13,5,30,22,3,13,5,9,22,16,10,1
120 DATAA  2 letters,B  3 letters,C  4 letters
130 DATAD  5 letters,E  Numbers to 10,F  Numbers to 20
140 DATAG  Tables to 4x,H  Tables to 8x,I  Tables to 12x
150 PS%=10:CS%=10:PROCGRAPH
160 RESTORE120:PRINTTAB(11,10);
170 PRINTCHR$136;CHR$135;"Please choose";CHR$137
180 FORX=1TO9:READQ$:PRINTTAB(11,12+X);CHR$135;Q$:NEXT
190 PRINTTAB(11,22);CHR$130;"Your choice?";
200 REPEAT:Q$=GET$:UNTIL Q$>="A" AND Q$<="I"
210 CH%=ASC(Q$)-64
220 VDU7:PROCCLR:RESTORE120
230 FORX=1TO CH%:READX$:NEXT
240 PRINTTAB(11,15);CHR$135;"How difficult?"
250 PRINTTAB(11,17);CHR$135;"from 1 (easy)"
260 PRINTTAB(11,18);CHR$135;"to 9 (hard)..."
270 PRINTTAB(11,22);CHR$130;"Your choice?";
280 REPEAT:D=GET:UNTIL D>48 AND D<=58
290 PROCCLR:VDU7:PRINTTAB(11,10);C$
300 D=D-48:X$=RIGHT$(X$,LEN(X$)-3)
310 PRINTTAB(11,13);CHR$130;"You have chosen"
320 PRINTTAB(11,15);CHR$135;X$
```

```
330 PRINTTAB(11,16);CHR$135;"Difficulty ";D
340 PRINTTAB(11,18);CHR$130;"OK? (Y-N)";
350 REPEAT:G$=GET$:UNTIL G$="Y"OR G$="N"
360 IFG$="N"PROCCLR:GOTO160
370 VDU7:PROCCLR
380 PRINTTAB(11,13);CHR$135;X$
390 PRINTTAB(11,14);CHR$135;"Difficulty ";D:D=600-D*63
400
410 REM - Game loop
420
430 PRINTTAB(11,10);CHR$135;CHR$136;"READY !";CHR$137
440 K=INKEY(300):*FX15
450 PRINTTAB(11,10);C$;TAB(16,10);CHR$135;"PLAY!":VDU7
460 PROCCHOICE:IF CH%>4 L%=Z%:I$=Z$:GOTO490
470 L%=RND(15):IFL%=L1%GOTO470
480 L1%=L%:FORX%=1TOL%:READ I$:NEXT
490 PROCDBL(2,6,135,I$+B$):K=INKEY(D)
500 IF L%=R% OR K<>-1 PROCCHECK:GOTO430
510 PROCCHOICE:IF CH%>4 R%=Z%:J$=Z$:GOTO540
520 R%=RND(15):IF R%=R1% GOTO520
530 R1%=R%:FORX%=1TOR%:READ J$:NEXT
540 PROCDBL(21,6,135,J$+B$):K=INKEY(D)
550 IF L%=R% OR K<>-1 PROCCHECK:GOTO430
560 GOTO460
570
580 DEFPROCCHECK
590 IFL%<>R%OR K=-1 GOTO610
600 T$="You got it!":PS%=PS%+1:CS%=CS%-1:GOTO640
610 IFL%=R%ANDK=-1 T$="I got it!":GOTO630
620 T$="Not the same."
630 PS%=PS%-1:CS%=CS%+1
640 PRINTTAB(11,10);CHR$135;T$:VDU7
650 PROCGRAPH:K=INKEY(300):*FX15
660 PRINTTAB(11,10);C$
670 IFPS%<>0 AND CS%<>0 ENDPROC
680 CLS:PROCTITLE("GAME OVER")
690 IF CS%=0 PROCDBL(12,12,131,"YOU WIN!"):PROCWARBLE:END
700 PROCDBL(12,12,131,"I WIN!")
710 FORX=1TO3:PROCBOING:NEXT:END
720
730 DEFPROCbox(X%,Y%,L%,H%,C%)
740 LOCALV%,W%,I%,J%
750 PRINTTAB(X%,Y%);
760 V%=VPOS:W%=POS
770 PRINTTAB(W%,V%-H%);CHR$(C%+144);"7";
780 FORI%=0TOL%+1:PRINT"£";:NEXT
790 PRINT"k":PRINTTAB(W%,V%+1);CHR$(C%+144);"u";
800 FORI%=0TOL%+1:PRINT"p";:NEXT
810 PRINT"z":FORJ%=V%-H%+1TOV%
820 PRINTTAB(W%,J%);CHR$(C%+144);"5":NEXT
830 FORJ%=V%-H%+1TOV%
840 PRINTTAB(W%+L%+3,J%);CHR$(C%+144);"j":NEXT
850 ENDPROC
860
```

```
 870 DEFPROCDBL(X%,Y%,C%,X$)
 880 PRINTTAB(X%,Y%);CHR$141;CHR$C%;X$
 890 PRINTTAB(X%,Y%+1);CHR$141;CHR$C%;X$:ENDPROC
 900
 910 DEFPROCTITLE(X$)
 920 PRINTCHR$132;STRING$(19,"Oo")
 930 PROCDBL((36-LEN(X$))/2,4,131,X$)
 940 PRINTCHR$132;STRING$(19,"Oo")
 950 ENDPROC
 960
 970 DEFPROCGRAPH
 980 FORX%=(23-CS%*.66)TO23:PRINTTAB(3,X%);CHR$145;GR$:NEXT
 990 PRINTTAB(3,23-CS%*.66);"   "
1000 FORX%=(23-PS%*.66)TO23:PRINTTAB(32,X%);CHR$147;GR$:NEXT
1010 PRINTTAB(32,23-PS%*.66);"   "
1020 PRINTTAB(3,3);CHR$135;CS%;" "
1030 PRINTTAB(32,3);CHR$135;PS%;" ":ENDPROC
1040
1050 DEFPROCCLR
1060 FORX%=13TO22:PRINTTAB(12,X%);C$:NEXT:ENDPROC
1070
1080 DATAit,to,at,on,in,by,be,me,my,up,an,am,as,is,so
1090 DATAbun,ban,bin,din,bed,bud,bid,did,dud,nod,and,den
1100 DATAboy,say,day,band,bend,bond,bind,dens,send,sand
1110 DATAnods,fire,find,fine,rind,rent,rend,tire
1120 DATAbrush,shrub,shred,sheds,stabs,drays,brays,burst
1130 DATAstrew,straw,stars,slabs,stubs,blest,blast
1140
1150 DEFPROCCHOICE
1160 REM - If the program is renumbered, the RESTORE
1170 REM - value of next line must be altered manually.
1180
1190 IFCH%<=4 RESTORE(1070+10*CH%):GOTO1320
1200 IFCH%>=7 GOTO1260
1210 IFRND(1)>.5 GOTO1240
1220 Z$=STR$(RND((CH%-3)*2))+" + "+STR$(RND((CH%-3)*2))
1230 Z%=EVAL(Z$):GOTO1320
1240 Z$=STR$(RND((CH%-3)*2)+RND((CH%-3)*2))
1250 Z%=EVAL(Z$):ENDPROC
1260 IFRND(1)>.5 GOTO1300
1270 Z$=STR$(RND(5)-1+(CH%-7)*4)
1280 Z$=Z$+" * "+STR$(RND(5)-1+(CH%-7)*4)
1290 Z%=EVAL(Z$):GOTO1320
1300 Z$=STR$((RND(5)-1+(CH%-7)*4)*(RND(5)-1+(CH%-7)*4))
1310 Z%=EVAL(Z$):GOTO1320
1320 ENDPROC
1330
1340 DEFPROCBOING
1350 SOUND 0,-15,80,2
1360 FOR S%=-15 TO 0:SOUND1,S%,20+S%,2:NEXT:ENDPROC
1370
1380 DEFPROCWARBLE
1390 FORS%=1TO20:SOUND1,-12,30,1
1400 SOUND1,-12,100,1:NEXT:ENDPROC
```

23

Pontoon

Everyone knows how to play Pontoon (or Vingt-et-un), so we need not waste time discussing it. In this computer version the user plays against the computer. Both start with £100 cash, and the bets are very simple; £1 per hand. You are not allowed to 'buy' another card, although some readers may wish to include this facility, by changing the procedure a little at PROCPPLAY.

The deck of cards is worth considering. It is contained in the array A(0) to A(51), with Hearts having values 0 to 12, Clubs from 13 to 25 and so on. Initially the deck is uncut – i.e. the cards are in order – and PROCSHUFFLE moves them around. We utilise a pointer called NXTCARD to indicate the next card to be dealt, and when NXTCARD equals 52 (off the end of the deck), it is set to 0 again. This means that once the deck has been shuffled, the cards are dealt infallibly in the same order. According to the 'letter of the law' this

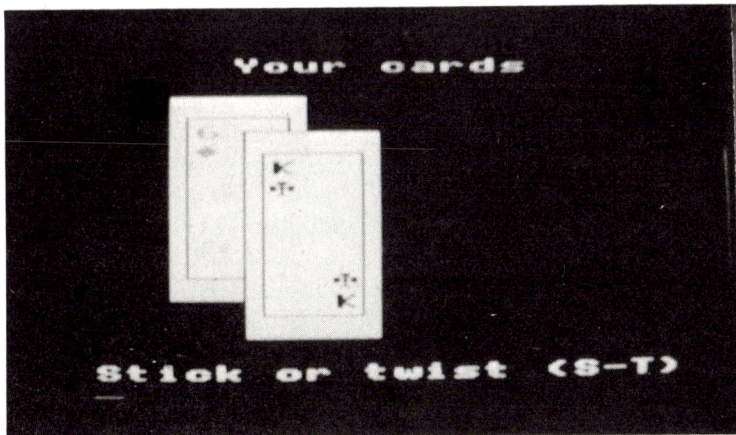

is right, but experience has shown that the situation can arise where a Pontoon call is impossible and so the deal never changes hands. (Besides, in the game as played entirely by humans, there is a slight rearrangement of cards as they are collected and placed at the bottom of the deck.) Therefore, I have arranged for the deck to be reshuffled whenever NXTCARD equals 52, as well as whenever there is a Pontoon call.

When the player peruses his or her own hand – as player or dealer – the cards are shown pictorially, as you will see from the illustration, and I have also arranged that the computer's hand is shown in those situations where it may be suspected that the computer is cheating or perhaps not functioning correctly. The displays are of course very similar, and the user must be aware of the text above the display, which lets you know whose hand is being shown.

The arrays P(5) and C(5) hold the undecoded card values held by the player and the computer respectively, and line 40 prepares the uncut deck. Lines 50 to 80 redefine four graphics symbols for Heart, Club, Diamond and Spade, and line 100 defines a text area at the bottom of the screen.

The game loop is easy to follow. B is the flag denoting who is the dealer, while PFLAG and CFLAG are the score values of the player's hand and the computer's hand respectively, where 0 = bust, 1 = stick, 3 = Pontoon and 5 = five-card trick.

PROCOMPLAY – the computer's play – starts with a call to PROCPREP, which prepares the screen. We then utilise function ADD, defined on lines 1540 to 1580, which decodes the card number held (0 to 51) to its value in Pontoon (1–11). The logic of computer choice, etc., follows. If the computer's hand is between 16 and 21, there is a mathematical choice in the equation of line 470, which makes the computer play a good game, but one that is not too predictable.

If the computer has bust – gone over 21 – lines 540 onwards check for the presence of an Ace. If one is found, the total is reduced by 10 in line 550, and the coded card number is made negative. This is so the card will still be displayed correctly, but it cannot again reduce the score by 10.

When it is the player's turn, line 620 calls PROCHAND, which displays the cards graphically. The two parameters passed to PROCHAND are (a) the number of the card in the hand – first, second, etc. – and (b) the code number of the card. Line 1320 calculates the position of the card on the screen, and then line 1330 defines the graphics area to be the position and size of the card and clears it to background black, in case it overlaps another card. Line 1340 redefines that area a little smaller and clears it in white, then lines 1350 and 1360 repeat the process. The result is a white playing card with a tiny black edge, inside it being a black line marking off a white margin. (See the illustration.)

Line 1370 decodes the card number to suit and value, and then E$ is loaded with the print equivalent. Finally, lines 1470 on print the suit symbol and the value in two places. If desired, users could extend this to have suit symbols printed the correct number of times – nine times on the nine of Hearts, for example – but in practice twice is quite enough.

You should be able to follow the rest of the listing quite easily.

Variables

PCASH	Player's cash
CCASH	Computer's cash
A(51)	The pack or deck of cards
P(5)	Player's coded card numbers
C(5)	Computer coded card numbers
Q$	General input string
B	Banker, where 0 = computer and 1 = player
PFLAG	Value of player's hand, where 0 = bust, etc.
CFLAG	Value of computer's hand
C	Counter when dealing cards
CD	Coded value of card dealt
CCARDS	Number of cards in computer's hand
PCARDS	Number of cards in player's hand
CTOT	Game value of computer's cards
PTOT	Game value of player's cards
X	General counter
G$	Dummy
S	Selected card whilst shuffling
Z	Temporary holding variable in exchanging
NXTCARD	Card next to be dealt, 0 to 51

In PROCHAND:

I%	Card in hand – first, second, etc.
V%	Coded number of card; then suit 0–3
A%	Position on screen of left edge
B%	Ditto, bottom edge
C%	Ditto, right edge
D%	Ditto, top edge
E%	Card value in suit, 0 (King) to 12 (Queen)
S$	Suit symbol, Heart, Club, Diamond, Spade
E$	Value 2 to 10, or initial, A, J, Q, K
P	Print offset to allow for 2-digit '10'

```
   10 MODE7:PROCTITLE("PONTOON")
   20 PCASH=100:CCASH=100:*FX11,0
   30 DIM A(51),P(5),C(5)
   40 FOR X=0 TO 51:A(X)=X:NEXT
   50 VDU23,224,54,127,127,127,62,28,8,0
   60 VDU23,225,28,28,107,127,107,8,28,0
   70 VDU23,226,8,28,62,127,62,28,8,0
   80 VDU23,227,8,28,62,127,127,107,8,0
   90 INPUT'''"Do you want the bank (Y-N)",Q$
  100 MODE5:VDU28,0,29,19,21:IF Q$="Y" B=1 ELSE B=0
  110 PROCSHUFFLE
  120
  130 REM - Game loop
  140
  150 REPEAT:CLS
  160 PROCDEAL:IF B=1 GOTO 190
  170 PROCPPLAY
  180 IF PFLAG=0 CFLAG=1:GOTO220
  190 PROCOMPLAY:IF B=0 GOTO220
  200 IF CFLAG=0 PFLAG=1:GOTO220
  210 PROCPPLAY
  220 PROCWINNER
  230 CLS:IF PFLAG<>3 AND CFLAG<>3 GOTO280
  240 PRINT"Pontoon"
  250 IF B=0 AND PFLAG=3 GOTO 270
  260 IF B=1 AND CFLAG<>3 GOTO 275
  270 PRINT"Deal changes.":B=1-B
  275 PROCSHUFFLE
  280 UNTIL PCASH=0 OR CCASH=0
  290 END
  300
  310 DEFPROCDEAL
  320 IF B PRINT"You deal.."ELSE PRINT"I deal.."
  330 FOR C=1 TO 2
  340 PROCGETCARD:P(C)=CD
  350 PROCGETCARD:C(C)=CD
  360 NEXT C:CCARDS=2:PCARDS=2
  370 ENDPROC
  380
  390 DEFPROCOMPLAY
  400 PROCPREP("")
  410 CTOT=FNADD(C(1))+FNADD(C(2))
  420 CLS:IF CCARDS<5 GOTO440
  430 PRINT"I have 5-card trick.":CFLAG=5:GOTO580
  440 IF CTOT<>21 OR CCARDS<>2 GOTO460
  450 PRINT"I have Pontoon.":CFLAG=3:GOTO580
  460 IF CTOT>21 GOTO540
  470 IF CTOT<16 OR RND(1)<(20-CTOT)/13 GOTO490
  480 PRINT"I stick.":CFLAG=1:GOTO580
  490 PRINT"I take a card.":PROCGETCARD
  500 CCARDS=CCARDS+1:C(CCARDS)=CD
  510 CTOT=CTOT+FNADD(CD)
  520 IF CTOT<=21 GOTO420
  530 REM - Over 21. Any Aces?
  540 FOR X=1 TO CCARDS
```

```
550 IF C(X)MOD13=1 C(X)=-C(X):CTOT=CTOT-10
560 NEXT X:IF CTOT<=21 GOTO420
570 PRINT;'"I bust with ";CTOT:CFLAG=0
580 PROCRET:ENDPROC
590
600 DEFPROCPPLAY
610 PROCPREP("Your cards")
620 FOR Z=1 TO 2:PROCHAND(Z,P(Z)):NEXT:PC=2
630 PTOT=FNADD(P(1))+FNADD(P(2))
640 VDU4:IF PTOT<16 GOTO700
650 IF PTOT=21 AND PC=2 PRINT"Pontoon!":PFLAG=3:GOTO800
660 COLOUR3:PRINT"Stick or twist (S-T)";
670 REPEAT:G$=GET$
680 UNTIL G$="T" OR G$="S" OR ASCG$=13
690 IF G$="S" OR ASCG$=13 PFLAG=1:GOTO810
700 PROCGETCARD:PC=PC+1:PROCHAND(PC,CD)
710 P(PC)=CD:PTOT=PTOT+FNADD(CD)
720 IF PTOT<=21 CLS:GOTO 780
730 REM Any Aces?
740 FOR X=1 TO PC
750 IF P(X)MOD13=1 P(X)=-P(X):PTOT=PTOT-10
760 NEXT:IF PTOT<=21 GOTO780
770 COLOUR1:PRINT"BUST!":PFLAG=0:GOTO800
780 IF PC=5 PRINT"5-CARD TRICK!":PFLAG=5:GOTO800
790 CLS:GOTO640
800 PRINT'"Press RETURN";:G$=GET$
810 ENDPROC
820
830 DEFPROCWINNER
835 IF PFLAG=5 OR CFLAG=5 S%=5 ELSE S%=2
840 CLS:IF PFLAG=0 GOTO960
850 PROCPREP("My cards")
860 FOR X%=1 TO CCARDS
870 PROCHAND(X%,C(X%)):NEXT
880 IF PFLAG>CFLAG GOTO940
890 IF CFLAG>PFLAG GOTO960
900 IF PTOT>CTOT GOTO940
910 IF CTOT>PTOT GOTO960
920 PRINT"Dealer wins ties."'
930 IF B=0 GOTO960
940 COLOUR2:PRINT"You win!"
950 PCASH=PCASH+S%:CCASH=CCASH-S%:GOTO980
960 COLOUR1:PRINT'"I win!"
970 PCASH=PCASH-S%:CCASH=CCASH+S%
980 COLOUR3
990 PRINT;'"CASH;"'"You - £";PCASH;" Me - £";CCASH
1000 PROCRET:ENDPROC
1010
1020 DEFPROCTITLE(X$)
1030 PRINTCHR$132;STRING$(19,"Oo")
1040 PROCDBL((36-LEN(X$))/2,3,131,X$)
1050 PRINT'CHR$132;STRING$(19,"Oo")
1060 ENDPROC
1070
1080 DEFPROCRET:COLOUR2
```

```
1090 PRINT'"Press RETURN ";:G$=GET$:CLS
1100 ENDPROC
1110
1120 DEFPROCDBL(X%,Y%,C%,X$)
1130 PRINTTAB(X%,Y%);CHR$C%;CHR$141;X$
1140 PRINTTAB(X%,Y%+1);CHR$C%;CHR$141;X$
1150 ENDPROC
1160
1170 DEFPROCSHUFFLE
1180 IF B PRINT"You shuffle.."ELSE PRINT"I shuffle..'
1190 FOR X=0 TO 51
1200 S=RND(52)-1:IF S=X GOTO1200
1210 Z=A(S):A(S)=A(X):A(X)=Z
1220 NEXT:NXTCARD=0:PROCRET
1230 ENDPROC
1240
1250 DEFPROCGETCARD
1260 CD=A(NXTCARD):NXTCARD=NXTCARD+1
1270 IF NXTCARD=52 NXTCARD=0:PROCSHUFFLE
1280 ENDPROC
1290
1300 DEFPROCHAND(I%,V%)
1310 LOCAL A%,B%,C%,D%,E%,P,E$,S$
1320 A%=I%*160:B%=400+72*(I%MOD2):C%=A%+300:D%=B%+400
1330 GCOL0,128:VDU24,A%;B%;C%;D%;16
1340 GCOL0,131:VDU24,A%+8;B%+4;C%-8;D%-4;16
1350 GCOL0,128:VDU24,A%+44;B%+44;C%-44;D%-44;16
1360 GCOL0,131:VDU24,A%+52;B%+48;C%-52;D%-48;16
1370 E%=ABS((V%)MOD13):V%=ABS((V%)DIV13)
1380 IF E%=1 E$="A":GOTO1430
1390 IF E%=0 E$="K":GOTO1430
1400 IF E%=11 E$="J":GOTO1430
1410 IF E%=12 E$="Q":GOTO1430
1420 E$=STR$E%
1430 IF V%=0 GCOL0,1:S$=CHR$224
1440 IF V%=1 GCOL0,0:S$=CHR$225
1450 IF V%=2 GCOL0,1:S$=CHR$226
1460 IF V%=3 GCOL0,0:S$=CHR$227
1470 VDU5:MOVEA%+52,B%+300:PRINTS$
1480 MOVEA%+186,B%+124:PRINTS$
1490 MOVEA%+56,B%+340:PRINTE$
1500 IF LEN(E$)=1 P=192 ELSE P=128
1510 MOVEA%+P,B%+84:PRINTE$
1520 VDU4:ENDPROC
1530
1540 DEF FNADD(A%)
1550 A%=A%MOD13
1560 IF A%=0 OR A%>=11 A%=10
1570 IF A%=1 A%=11
1580 =A%
1590
1600 DEFPROCPREP(X$)
1610 VDU26,18,0,128,16,28,0,29,19,21,5,18,0,2
1620 MOVE300,950:PRINTX$:VDU4:ENDPROC
```

24

Scribble

Scribble is a game for any number of players up to six, and has much in common with Scrabble, Lexicon and similar word games. The object is to make words, for which the computer awards points, the first player reaching a score of 200 points being the winner.

On his or her turn, the player may do one of three things: (a) shuffle the letter pool, (b) take a letter from the pool and add it to his hand, or (c) make a word from the letters in his hand. To shuffle the pool, the player simply presses RETURN. To take up a letter from the pool, the letter is typed. The computer removes the letter from the pool and adds it to those in the player's hand, then selects another letter for the pool. To play a word, the player types the

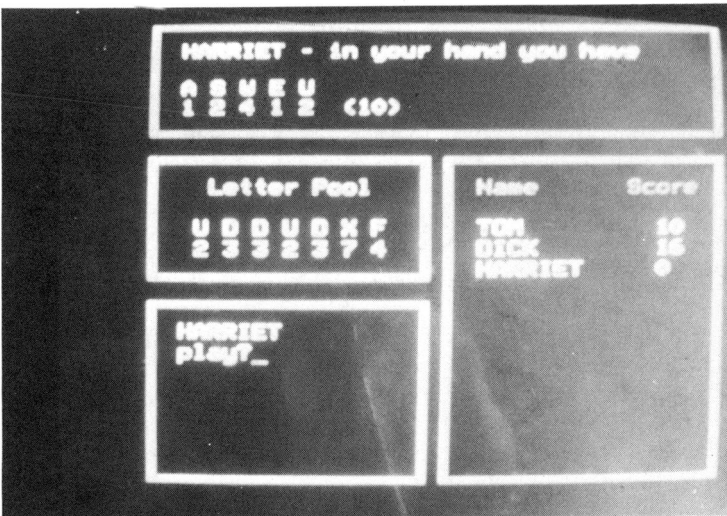

whole word and presses RETURN. The computer checks that the word is possible from the letters in the hand, and if so, asks if any other player objects to the word or to its spelling. If all is well, the score is calculated and the letters are removed from the player's hand.

Please note very carefully that the score for a word depends upon (a) the individual values of the letters making up the word, (b) the length of the word, with longer words scoring heavily, and (c) the number of letters remaining in the hand; the more letters left unused, the greater the penalty. At the extreme, it is just possible to play a short word, have a lot of letters left over and so be awarded a negative score!

There are 'jokers' in the form of '*', which have no value but which may be used in place of any letter. To pick up such a joker, the '*' must be typed. On the other hand, to play a word containing a joker, the player does not include '*', but types the whole word as he or she wishes it to be. The computer first checks for normal letters and if one or more short, checks for jokers.

Before and after each player's move there is a timed delay for thought and observation, but players may move the game on swiftly by pressing RETURN. Finally, the number of times that each player may shuffle the letter pool is limited, dependent upon the number of players.

Lines 30 to 50 scatter various letters around the screen in a variety of colours and may well be omitted. They just make a pretty introduction to the game. The title screen appears on lines 60 to 80 and is moved on automatically after five seconds, or sooner if desired by pressing any key. The next lines seek information on the number of players, calculate the number of times each may shuffle the letter pool, and seek players' names. We then call PROCDIS-PLAY which in turn calls PROCBOX several times, creating an attractive playing screen. PROCINIT selects a starting pool of seven letters and also selects five letters for each player. We then enter the game loop.

It will be seen that the game loop is very simple. On each pass through it will call PROCPLAY, PROCPOOL, PROCPANEL and PROC2 before checking if the current player PL% has reached a winning score.

PROCPLAY calls PROCPANEL, which prints the player's name and lists the letters in his or her hand, with values printed below. The player is then prompted for his play, in line 1020. If G$ is empty, RETURN has been pressed on an empty set and so the player wants to shuffle the letter pool. If the length of the input string is 1, the player wishes to take a letter from the pool, and this is checked on line 1090. The presence of the letter in the pool is looked for in line 1120 and, all being well, line 1180 takes it into the player's hand. A new letter for the pool is found in line 1200.

The player's hand is checked, in lines 1220 onward, when he wishes to make a word. Each character of the input string is checked against the letters held, but notice that in order to save memory space we save the ASCII value of the letters, not the letters themselves. If we are short of a letter or two, lines 1300 to 1310 check for the presence of a joker. We have kept a running score of letter values in T% while the checking was going on, and in line 1440 we add a bonus for the length of the word and subtract three points for each letter left in the hand. Change this if you don't like it. The rest of the listing should be fairly straightforward.

You will see that the values of the 26 letters are stored as DATA statements in line 710, with the most commonly used letters having a value of 1, rising up to 9 for Q and Z. The letters themselves are held in lines 720 to 800, and at first sight one might wonder why they are there at all – why not just pick a random number 1 to 26? In practice, however, such a course would have the J, X or Z occurring as often as E or A; clearly not a desirable state of affairs. Of course, one could write a RND statement and hedge it about with all sorts of IFs and other things to increase the frequency of chosen letters, but in the end one has a whole lot of BASIC statements that take up far more space than the DATA lines shown. I wrote the alphabet several times and then altered infrequently occurring letters to others over a large number of games until I achieved what I thought to be the right mix. Change it by all means!

Variables

C$	Row of spaces for clearance purposes
X%	General counter
C%	Random colour
Q$	General-purpose print string; also dummy
P%	Number of players
MAX%	Shuffles permitted per player
P%(X,Y)	Player's data, where X = player number and Y = 0 = score Y = 1 to 12 = ASCII value of letters held Y = 13 = shuffles used
P$(X)	Players' names
POOL$	Letters in pool
C%(X)	Current player's letters
PL%	Currrent player number

In PROCINIT:

X%	General counter
L%	Randomly chosen letter, 1 to 178
G$	Chosen letter

In PROCPOOL:

X%	General counter
V%	Letter value
C%	Alphabetic position
A%	General counter

In PROCPLAY:

G$	Player's input
X$	Message string
Q$	Dummy
X%	General counter
Y%	Number of first empty place in player's hand
C%	Randomly chosen letter
T%	Running total of score
Z%	General counter
S%	Letter value

```
 10 REM - Scribble
 20 C$=STRING$(15," ")
 30 CLS:FORX%=1 TO 200:C%=RND(26)+64
 40 Q$=CHR$(RND(7)+128)+CHR$C%
 50 PRINTTAB(RND(37),RND(22));Q$:NEXT
 60 PROCDBL(12,3,135,"SCRIBBLE    ")
 70 PRINTTAB(13);"                "
 80 PROCDBL(2,9,135," THE  COMPUTER  WORD  GAME  ")
 90 Q$=INKEY$(500):MODE7
100 PRINT''''"How many players (1-6)";:PROCBOX(1,1,4)
110 REPEAT:P%=GET-48:UNTIL P%>0 AND P%<=6:PRINT;P%
120 MAX%=12/(P%+1)
130 IF P%=1 PRINT''"You";ELSE PRINT''"Each player";
140 PRINT;" may shuffle the letters"
150 IF MAX%=1 PRINT"once."''ELSE PRINT;MAX%;" times."''
160 INPUT" Press RETURN..."G$
170 DIM P%(P%,13),P$(P%),POOL$(7),C%(12)
180 CLS:FOR X%=1 TO P%
190 PRINT'"Player #";X%;" -"
200 PRINT"please type your name ";:PROCBOX(12,1,4)
210 INPUT P$(X%):NEXT:PROCDISPLAY:PROCINIT:PL%=1
220
230 REM - GAME LOOP ***************
240
250 PROCPLAY
260 PROCPOOL
```

```
270 PROCPANEL
280 PROCCL2
290 IF P%(PL%,0)<200 PL%=(PL%MODP%)+1:GOTO250
300 PRINTTAB(21,19);CHR$135;CHR$136;P$(PL%);" WINS!";
310 END
320
330 DEFPROCDBL(X%,Y%,C%,X$)
340 PRINTTAB(X%,Y%);CHR$141;CHR$C%;X$
350 PRINTTAB(X%,Y%+1);CHR$141;CHR$C%;X$:ENDPROC
360
370 DEFPROCBOX(L%,H%,C%)
380 V%=VPOS:W%=POS
390 PRINTTAB(W%,V%-H%);CHR$(C%+144);"7";
400 FOR I%=0 TO L%+1:PRINT"£";:NEXT:PRINT"k"
410 PRINTTAB(W%,V%+1);CHR$(C%+144);"u";
420 FOR I%=0 TO L%+1:PRINT"p";:NEXT:PRINT"z"
430 FOR J%=V%-H%+1 TO V%
440 PRINTTAB(W%,J%);CHR$(C%+144);"5";CHR$135:NEXT
450 FOR J%=V%-H%+1 TO V%
460 PRINTTAB(W%+L%+3,J%);CHR$(C%+144);"j":NEXT
470 PRINTTAB(W%+3,V%);"";:ENDPROC
480
490 DEFPROCDISPLAY
500 CLS:PRINTTAB(0,4);:PROCBOX(35,4,1)
510 PRINTTAB(0,11);:PROCBOX(15,4,3)
520 PRINTTAB(4,8);CHR$133;"Letter Pool"
530 PRINTTAB(20,21);:PROCBOX(15,14,2)
540 PRINTTAB(22,8);CHR$129;"Name        Score"
550 PRINTTAB(0,21);:PROCBOX(15,7,4)
560 ENDPROC
570
580 DEFPROCINIT
590 PROCMIX:REM - Shuffle pool
600 FOR X%=1 TO P%:FOR C%=1 TO 5
610 RESTORE 720:L%=RND(178)
620 FOR Y%=1 TO L%:READ G$:NEXT
630 P%(X%,C%)=ASC(G$):NEXT:NEXT
640 PROCUPDATE:PROCPOOL:ENDPROC
650
660 DEFPROCMIX:REM - Shuffle pool
670 FOR X%=1 TO 7:RESTORE 720
680 L%=RND(178)
690 FOR Y%=1 TO L%:READ POOL$(X%)
700 NEXT:NEXT:ENDPROC
710 DATA 1,5,3,3,1,4,2,2,1,6,5,2,3,3,1,3,9,3,2,2,2,6,4,7,2,9
720 DATA A,B,C,D,E,F,E,E,I,J,K,L,E,A,O,P,*,R,S,T,U
730 DATA V,I,X,Y,U,A,B,C,D,E,F,G,H,I,J,K,L,M,N,O,P
740 DATA O,R,S,T,U,V,A,X,Y,E,A,B,C,D,E,F,G,H,I,E,*
750 DATA L,M,N,O,P,R,S,T,U,E,W,X,Y,A,B,C,D,E,F,G,H
760 DATA I,J,K,L,M,N,O,P,R,S,T,U,E,W,Y,*
770 DATA A,B,C,D,E,F,G,H,I,E,L,M,N,O,P,R,S,T,E,W,Y,*
780 DATA A,C,D,E,F,G,H,I,L,E,N,O,P,R,S,T,U,W,Y,*
790 DATA A,C,D,E,G,H,I,L,M,N,O,P,R,S,T,U,Y,*,A,E,G
800 DATA H,I,L,M,O,S,T,U,Y,*,A,E,I,O,E
810
```

```
 820 DEFPROCUPDATE:REM - Print scores
 830 FOR X%=1 TO P%
 840 PRINTTAB(22,9+X%);CHR$135;P$(X%);TAB(35,9+X%);P%(X%,0)
 850 NEXT:ENDPROC
 860
 870 DEFPROCPOOL:REM - Print pool
 880 PRINTTAB(3,10);CHR$135;
 890 FOR X%=1 TO 7:PRINT;POOL$(X%);" ";:NEXT
 900 PRINTTAB(3,11);CHR$134;
 910 FOR X%=1 TO 7:IF POOL$(X%)="*" V%=0:GOTO950
 920 C%=ASC(POOL$(X%))-64
 930 RESTORE 710
 940 FOR A%=1 TO C%:READ V%:NEXT
 950 PRINT;V%;" ";
 960 NEXT:ENDPROC
 970
 980 DEFPROCPLAY
 990 *FX15,1
1000 PROCPANEL:VDU7
1010 PRINTTAB(2,15);CHR$135;P$(PL%);
1020 PRINTTAB(2,16);CHR$135;"play";:INPUT G$
1030 IF G$<>""GOTO1090
1040 IF P%(PL%,13)<MAX% GOTO1080
1050 X$="All shuffles used"
1060 PRINTTAB(2,17);CHR$129;X$
1070 PROCBOING:Q$=INKEY$(500):PROCCLIP:GOTO990
1080 PROCMIX:PROCPOOL:ENDPROC
1090 IF LEN(G$)>1 GOTO1220 ELSE X%=1
1100
1110 REM - Take letter from pool
1120 IF POOL$(X%)=G$ GOTO1150
1130 X%=X%+1:IF X%<=7 GOTO1120
1140 X$="Not in the pool":GOTO1060
1150 IF P%(PL%,12)<>0 X$="Hand full":GOTO1060
1160 Y%=1
1170 IF P%(PL%,Y%)<>0 Y%=Y%+1:GOTO1170
1180 P%(PL%,Y%)=ASC(G$)
1190 RESTORE 720:C%=RND(178)
1200 FOR D%=1 TO C%:READ POOL$(X%):NEXT:ENDPROC
1210
1220 REM - Make a word
1230 FOR X%=1 TO 12:C%(X%)=P%(PL%,X%):NEXT:FL%=1
1240 T%=0:FOR X%=1 TO LEN(G$)
1250 C%=ASC(MID$(G$,X%,1)):Y%=1
1260 IF C%=C%(Y%) GOTO1320 ELSE Y%=Y%+1
1270 IF Y%<=12 GOTO1260 ELSE Y%=1
1280
1290 REM - Letter not found. Check *'s
1300 IF C%(Y%)=42 GOTO1320 ELSE Y%=Y%+1
1310 IF Y%<=12 GOTO1300 ELSE X$="Impossible":GOTO1060
1320 C%(Y%)=0:IF C%(Y%)=42 GOTO1340
1330 RESTORE 710:FOR Z%=1 TO C%-64:READ S%:NEXT
1340 T%=T%+S%:NEXT X%
1350 PRINTTAB(2,17);CHR$130;"Objections? ";
1360 REPEAT:Q$=GET$:UNTIL Q$="Y" OR Q$="N":PRINTQ$
```

```
1370 IF Q$<>"Y"GOTO1430
1380 P%(PL%,0)=P%(PL%,0)-10:PROCCLIP
1390 PRINTTAB(2,16);CHR$129;"Penalty 10"
1400 Q$=INKEY$(500):PROCCLIP:GOTO1010
1410
1420 REM - Calculate score
1430 C%=0:FOR X%=1 TO 12:IF C%(X%)<>0 C%=C%+1
1440 NEXT X%:T%=T%+(LEN(G$)-1)↑2-C%
1450 P%(PL%,0)=P%(PL%,0)+T%
1460 PRINTTAB(2,18);CHR$133;"Score ";T%
1470 PROCUPDATE:PROCWARBLE:PROCCL2:Y%=1
1480 FOR X%=1 TO 12:P%(PL%,X%)=0:NEXT
1490 FOR X%=1 TO 12
1500 IF C%(X%)=0 GOTO1520
1510 P%(PL%,Y%)=C%(X%):Y%=Y%+1
1520 NEXT X%
1530 ENDPROC
1540
1550 DEFPROCPANEL:REM - Player's panel
1560 PROCCL3
1570 PRINTTAB(2,1);CHR$135;P$(PL%);
1580 PRINT" - in your hand you have"
1585 PRINTTAB(2,3);CHR$135;:X%=1
1590 IF P%(PL%,X%)=0 GOTO1620
1600 PRINT;CHR$(P%(PL%,X%));" ";
1610 X%=X%+1:IF X%<=12 GOTO1600
1620 PRINTTAB(2,4);CHR$134;:X%=1:T%=0
1630 IF P%(PL%,X%)=0 GOTO1680
1640 IF P%(PL%,X%)=42 V%=0:GOTO1670
1650 RESTORE 710
1660 FOR A%=1 TO P%(PL%,X%)-64:READ V%:NEXT
1670 PRINT;V%;" ";:T%=T%+V%:X%=X%+1:IF X%<=12 GOTO1630
1680 PRINT;" (";T%;")":ENDPROC
1690
1700 DEFPROCCLIP:REM Clear input
1710 PRINTTAB(2,16);C$:PRINTTAB(3,17);C$:ENDPROC
1720 DEFPROCCL2:REM Clear input panel
1730 G$=INKEY$(500)
1740 FOR X%=15 TO 18:PRINTTAB(3,X%);C$:NEXT:ENDPROC
1750 DEFPROCCL3:REM Clear player's panel
1760 FORX%=1 TO 4:PRINTTAB(2,X%);STRING$(36," "):NEXT
1770 ENDPROC
1780
1790 DEFPROCWARBLE
1800 FORS%=1TO20:SOUND1,-12,30,1
1810 SOUND1,-12,100,1:NEXT:ENDPROC
1820
1830 DEFPROCBOING
1840 SOUND 0,-15,80,2
1850 FOR S%=-15 TO 0:SOUND1,S%,20+S%,2:NEXT:ENDPROC
```

25

Cape Horn

This is another action game, but one that will appeal more to thinkers, for it simulates the problems of taking a sailing ship east to west around Cape Horn, against the prevailing winds. The title page asks the user to choose a difficulty level from 1 to 6:

Level 1. At this level the wind is steady in both strength and direction and round the Horn is simply a matter of tacking once or twice.

Level 2. For this level, the wind stays constant in force, but changes direction randomly, veering or backing a few degrees at a time.

Level 3. Now the wind also changes velocity, from Force 1 on the Beaufort scale to Force 12 (hurricane).

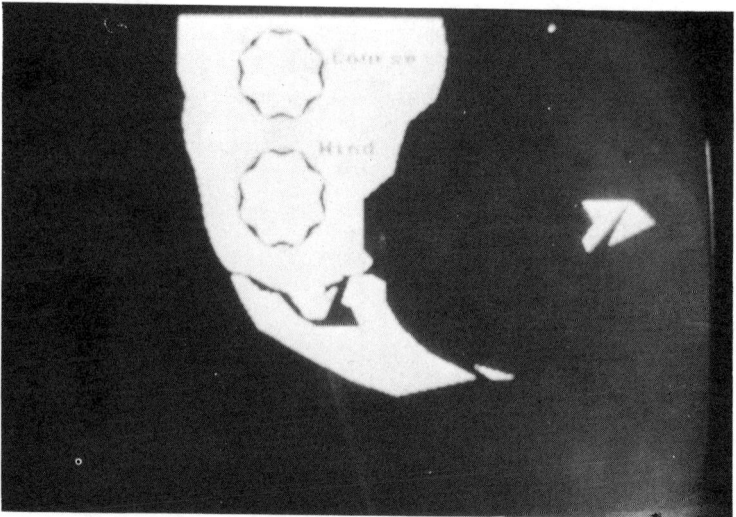

Level 4. As above, but the Antarctic pack ice encroaches on the sea lane a little, reducing the space for manoeuvre.
Level 5. As above, but more so.
Level 6. As above, but in addition icebergs are scattered randomly.

After the user has given his or her choice of difficulty level, a very brief message on the lines of the explanations above is given to remind him of what to expect. Pressing RETURN moves the program on.

The screen clears and in its place is given a map of Cape Horn from about 49 degrees South to just above the South Shetland Islands, and from 67 West to 77 West, taking in the Falkland Islands. The map is of course only a representation, with the main channel of the Straits of Magellan indicated. The west coast here is a maze of small islands and no attempt has been made to indicate this.

On the mainland two compass roses are shown. One indicates the wind direction and the other the ship's course. There is a numeric indication of wind strength, but for the sake of simplicity the ship's speed is constant.

The ship appears as a small flashing dot somewhere north of the Falklands and the player's task is to manoeuvre it to the upper left of the screen and off the edge. The program will not allow the dot to disappear off right or left, and if it is brought up against these edges it will stay there. On the other hand, if the ship is taken off the bottom of the screen, it is assumed lost in the pack ice.

The player has only two controls, the P and S keys (short for Port and Starboard). All other keys are ignored. Note that port and starboard apply when facing forward on the ship, so that if the ship's course is south, port is on the player's right as he views the screen, whereas if the ship is going north, port is on the player's left. To operate, simply hold down the key for as long as desired. Course adjustments are in increments of 10 degrees.

The wind compass-rose indicator shows the direction of the wind in the same way that a burgee (a long narrow flag) would; by indicating the compass direction *to which* the wind is blowing. It used to be said that a finely rigged ship could sail within a few degrees of the wind on either tack, but of course as the wind rose, conditions on board would become more and more intolerable and almost suicidal. In high winds, reaching (or sailing at 90 degrees to the wind) would also be dangerous because of the possibility of being swamped by a sea, while in gales or hurricanes ships could do little but run before the wind.

These conditions have been simplified for the game in the following way. (a) Where the wind strength is 8 or less, the ship can be steered to within 45 degrees of the wind. (b) For a wind strength of 9, 90 degrees is the closest that one may reach. (c) For a strength of 10 or 11, the ship must run before the wind, with a 10 degree latitude. (d) With a wind strength of 12 the latitude is reduced to 5 degrees (see the diagram).

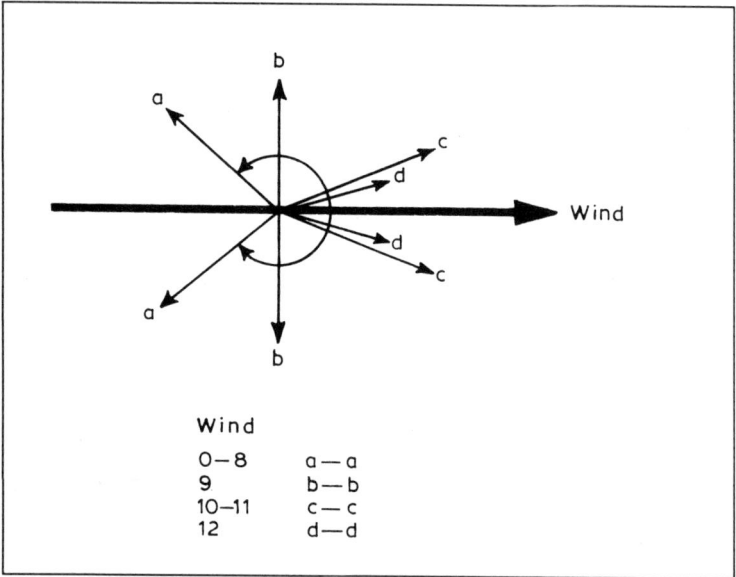

b

a

c

d

Wind

d

a

c

b

Wind

0–8	a — a
9	b — b
10–11	c — c
12	d — d

The mean strength of the wind is 6, with variations between 12 and 2. If – or when – it does drop to 2 or less, watch out! It will return a moment later with increased force and from a totally different direction. Getting your ship round the Horn is not easy!

The program will not allow you to sail closer to the wind than specified, but there are problems. Normally, while sailing close to the wind, if one wished to proceed on the other tack one would turn the bows through the eye of the wind, swing the boom over and proceed. Since in this game the wind can change direction, it is possible that while sailing close-hauled, one suddenly finds that one has changed tack unwittingly. This is a natural result of the above: the wind has changed a few degrees, forcing the computer to change the ship's heading. As with any new simulation, it's all quite logical when you get to know it.

The initial conditions are established in lines 110 to 130, with the wind strength = 6, direction = 80, desired course = 170 and the ship's position randomly determined within certain limits. PROC-SETCOURSE determines the ship's actual course (as distinct from desired) and then the map is drawn in PROCMAP. It does this with a judicious mix of DRAWing and PLOTting from DATA statements, drawing a series of various triangles north to south, adding triangles for a few islands, and then drawing the Magellan Straits as another series of triangles from west to east. Calls to PROCCIRC draw the compass roses. They are labelled and then the indicator needles are drawn. Finally, PROCMAP draws in a jagged series of triangles to represent icebergs, if the difficulty level requires it.

Back at line 150, a call to PROCSEA sets in train a continuing sound of crashing waves and howling wind. These are both interesting; the former because of the interesting shape of the ENVELOPE, and the fact that the driving channel 1 is not sounded. That is to say, the ENVELOPE affects channel 1 silently, but in turn it affects the noise channel 0. Channels 2 and 3 are slightly off-key with each other – and out of synchronisation with channel 1 – so the perceived tone has that mournful hollow sound one associates with wind.

In the game loop, at each pass the wind is adjusted for strength and direction, and if the strength jumps abruptly (line 250), a brief beep warns the user. Line 330 calls PROCSETCOURSE, which is a very complex procedure that adjusts the vessel's actual course, bearing in mind the wind direction and strength, and desired course. Readers are warned to copy this procedure extremely carefully, as it is naturally the very heart of the program and the slightest error will affect the correct operation of the program.

Line 350 adjusts the compass-rose pointers and then lines 400 to 430 calculate the ship's new position. Line 470 checks the colour of this point on the screen, calling PROCDONE if necessary. This procedure tells the user what has happened to his ship, or congratulates him on winning.

If the game is not over, line 560 accepts the user's input and adjusts the desired course or not as appropriate.

Variables

LVL%	Difficulty level
WIND%	Wind direction
DESCS%	Desired course, 0 to 360
SX%	X co-ordinate of ship's position
SY%	Y co-ordinate of ship's position
T%	Turns since last wind change
STR	Wind strength
W%	Wind direction – copy
S%	Wind strength – copy

C%	Copy of COURSE%
COURSE%	Current ship's heading, 0 to 360
NX%	Ship's next X co-ordinate
NY%	Ship's next Y co-ordinate
CX%, CY%	Looking further ahead
Q%	Colour of next point
I%	Player's input
G%	Dummy
D%	Course deviation allowed
F%	Course deviation desired
D1%, D2%	Permitted window

```
 10 MODE7:PROCTITLE("CAPE HORN")
 20 PRINT'';"Difficulty 1-6? ";
 30 REPEAT:LVL%=GET-48
 40 UNTIL LVL%>=1 AND LVL%<=6:PRINTLVL%
 50 PRINTTAB(0,13);:ONLVL%GOTO60,70,80,90,90,100
 60 PRINT"Wind steady throughout.":GOTO110
 70 PRINT"Wind changing in direction.":GOTO110
 80 PRINT"Wind increasing/decreasing, changing.":GOTO110
 90 PRINT"Ice pack encroaching on sea lane.":GOTO110
100 PRINT"Watch out for icebergs!"
110 WIND%=80:DESCS%=170:SX%=800+RND(400)
120 SY%=800+RND(200):T%=0:STR=6
140 PROCSETCOURSE
150 PROCRET:MODE1:PROCMAP:PROCSEA
160 VDU26,5:MOVESX%,SY%:PRINT"."
170 VDU19,3,8,0,0,0
180
190 REM - Game loop
200
210 W%=WIND%:S%=STR
220 IFLVL%>=2WIND%=WIND%+(RND(3)-2)*4
230 T%=T%+1:IF LVL%<3 OR T%<5 GOTO330
240 T%=0:IFSTR>2 GOTO260
250 STR=RND(6)+6:PROCWARN:WIND%=RND(360):GOTO290
260 IF RND(1)<=(0.95-LVL%/60) GOTO280
270 STR=STR+RND(8):PROCWARN:GOTO290
280 IFSTR<7 STR=STR+RND(3)-2 ELSE STR=STR-1
290 IFSTR>12 STR=10
300
310 REM - ADJUST DISPLAY
320
330 C%=COURSE%:PROCSETCOURSE
340 IFW%=WIND%GOTO360
350 PROCPT(450,650,W%):PROCPT(450,650,WIND%)
360 IFC%=COURSE%GOTO380
370 PROCPT(450,900,C%):PROCPT(450,900,COURSE%)
380 VDU26:IF S%=STR GOTO400
390 MOVE570,720:PRINT;S%:MOVE570,720:PRINT;INT(STR)
```

```
400 NX%=SX%+SIN(RAD(COURSE%))*6
410 CX%=SX%+SIN(RAD(COURSE%))*12
420 CY%=SY%+COS(RAD(COURSE%))*12
430 NY%=SY%+COS(RAD(COURSE%))*6
440
450 REM - CHECK FOR END
460
470 Q%=POINT(CX%+12,CY%-24):IF Q%=0 GOTO520
480 PROCDONE:IF FLAG%=0 GOTO560
490 MODE7:PROCDBL(0,5,131,Q$):Q%=INKEY(100)
500 *FX15,0
510 END
520 VDU26:MOVESX%,SY%:PRINT"."
530 MOVENX%,NY%:PRINT".":SX%=NX%:SY%=NY%
540
550 REM - PLAYER'S ADJUSTMENT
560 I%=INKEY(0):*FX15,1
570 IF I%=80 DESCS%=(DESCS%+350)MOD360:GOTO590
580 IFI%=83 DESCS%=(DESCS%+10)MOD360
590 G%=INKEY(100):GOTO210
600
610 REM -PROCEDURES BEGIN
620
630 DEFPROCSETCOURSE
640 LOCALD1%,D2%,F%
650 IFSTR<=8D%=135:GOTO670
660 IFSTR=9D%=90ELSEIFSTR=10D%=45ELSED%=15
670 F%=ABS(DESCS%-WIND%)
680 D1%=360-F%:IF D1%<F% F%=D1%
690 IF F%<D% COURSE%=DESCS%:GOTO800
700 IFSTR<=8GOTO740
710 IFABS(DESCS%-D1%)<ABS(DESCS%-D2%)COURSE%=WIND%+D%:GOTO730
720 COURSE%=WIND%-D%
730 GOTO800
740 IFI%<>80 AND I%<>83 GOTO780
750 IFI%=80COURSE%=(WIND%+F%-5)MOD360:GOTO800
760 IFI%=83COURSE%=(WIND%-F%+365)MOD360
770 GOTO800
780 IF RND(1)>.5 I%=80 ELSE I%=83
790 GOTO670
800 DESCS%=COURSE%
810 ENDPROC
820
830 DEFPROCTITLE(X$)
840 PRINTCHR$132;STRING$(19,"Oo")
850 PROCDBL((36-LEN(X$))/2,4,131,X$)
860 PRINTCHR$132;STRING$(19,"Oo")
870 ENDPROC
880
890 DEFPROCDBL(X%,Y%,C%,X$)
900 PRINTTAB(X%,Y%);CHR$141;CHR$C%;X$
910 PRINTTAB(X%,Y%+1);CHR$141;CHR$C%;X$:ENDPROC
920
930 DEFPROCRET
940 PRINTTAB(5,19);CHR$131;"Press";
```

```
 950 PRINTCHR$132;CHR$157;CHR$129;"RETURN   ";CHR$156;
 960 G$=GET$:ENDPROC
 970
 980 DEFPROCMAP
 990 VDU19,0,132,0,0,0,16:GCOL0,2
1000 MOVE800,1023:MOVE230,1023
1010 FORY=950TO300STEP-50:READA,B
1020 PLOT85,A,Y:PLOT85,B,Y
1030 NEXT
1040 PLOT85,700,270:MOVE870,320:MOVE900,300
1050 PLOT85,940,300:MOVE1100,640:MOVE1200,640
1060 PLOT85,1130,600:PLOT85,1110,550
1070 PLOT85,1100,570:MOVE1160,560
1080 MOVE1210,640:PLOT85,1260,600
1090 GCOL0,0:MOVE320,520:MOVE320,500
1100 FOR I%=340TO680STEP20:READJ%:PLOT85,I%,J%:NEXT
1110 MOVE520,400:MOVE620,400:PLOT85,600,440
1120 PLOT85,540,460:MOVE540,480:PLOT85,600,500:PLOT85,660,520
1130 GCOL0,0:VDU5
1140 PROCCIRC(450,900):PROCCIRC(450,650)
1150 VDU26:MOVE 560,950:PRINT"Course"
1160 MOVE 530,760:PRINT;"Wind"
1170 GCOL4,0:MOVE 570,720:PRINT;INT(STR)
1180 PROCPT(450,900,COURSE%):PROCPT(450,650,WIND%)
1190 IFLVL%<4 ENDPROC
1200 VDU26:GCOL0,2:MOVE0,0
1210 FORX%=0TO1279STEP10:PLOT85,X%,RND(50):NEXT
1220 IFLVL%<5 GOTO1300
1230 MOVE0,50:MOVE0,100
1240 FORX%=0TO1279STEP10:PLOT85,X%,RND(70)+50:NEXT
1250 IFLVL%<6 GOTO1300
1260 FORF%=1 TO RND(8)+12
1270 VDU29,RND(1279);RND(150)+100;
1280 MOVE0,0:MOVE0,0
1290 FORG%=1TORND(10):PLOT85,G%*10,RND(50):NEXT:NEXT
1300 GCOL4,0:ENDPROC
1310
1320 DATA810,230,800,230,780,250,720,240,700,250,690
1330 DATA270,620,280,620,290,620,310,670,340,670,370
1340 DATA700,400,760,500,860,600,510,500,500,470,480
1350 DATA460,470,420,420,400,416,400,500,500,500,500,540,480
1360
1370 DEFPROCCIRC(I%,J%)
1380 VDU29,I%;J%;:MOVE100,0
1390 FORP=0TORAD360STEPRAD15
1400 X%=100*COSP:Y%=100*SINP
1410 PLOT5,X%,Y%:NEXT
1420 FORP=0TORAD360STEPRAD45
1430 X%=80*COSP:Y%=80*SINP
1440 MOVEX%,Y%
1450 MOVE 100*COS(P-RAD22),100*SIN(P-RAD22)
1460 PLOT85,100*COS(P+RAD22),100*SIN(P+RAD22)
1470 NEXT:ENDPROC
1480
1490 DEFPROCPT(I%,J%,P%)
```

```
1500 VDU29,I%;J%;
1510 MOVE80*SIN(RADP%),80*COS(RADP%):DRAW0,0:ENDPROC
1520
1530 DEFPROCDONE
1540 FLAG%=0:IFQ%<>-1GOTO1580
1550 IF SY%<50 Q$="Lost in the Antarctic ice!":GOTO1630
1560 IF(SY%>200 AND SX%>300)OR(SX%<12 AND SY%<900)ENDPROC
1570 Q$="You win!":FLAG%=1:ENDPROC
1580 IFSX%>1000Q$="Wrecked on the Falkland Islands!":GOTO1630
1590 IFSY%<300 Q$="Struck an ice floe!":GOTO1630
1600 IF SY%<500 Q$="Wrecked on Tierra del Fuego!":GOTO1630
1610 IFSX%<500 Q$="Wrecked on the coast of Chile!":GOTO1630
1620 Q$="Wrecked on the coast of Argentina!"
1630 FLAG%=-1:ENDPROC
1640
1650 DEFPROCSEA
1660 ENVELOPE1,4,2,-2,-1,255,100,255,0,0,0,0,0,0
1670 ENVELOPE2,6,1,-1,0,80,80,20,12,-27,0,-12,50,50
1680 ENVELOPE3,6,1,-1,0,80,80,20,12,-27,0,-12,50,50
1690 SOUND1,1,255,255:SOUND0,-12,7,255
1700 SOUND2,2,20,255:SOUND3,3,54,255
1710 ENDPROC
1720
1730 DEFPROCWARN
1740 *FX15,0
1750 VDU7:SOUND1,1,255,255:SOUND0,-12,7,255
1760 SOUND2,2,20,255:SOUND3,3,54,255:ENDPROC
```

26

Reverse Polish calculator

Reverse Polish notation is a method of working complex mathematical formulae, invented a long time ago by a Polish mathematician. Of course, that introduction will immediately put off a lot of people – but don't let it! For one thing, Reverse Polish Notation – or RPN for short – is so easy to understand that after a few minutes of working with this calculator, you'll wonder why RPN isn't in wide use. For another, it is enormously useful and cuts out all of those horrendous-looking brackets that you see in formulae. Finally, this program will provide you with a very useful calculator – and one that not only offers calculating ability, but will also offer help if you need it!

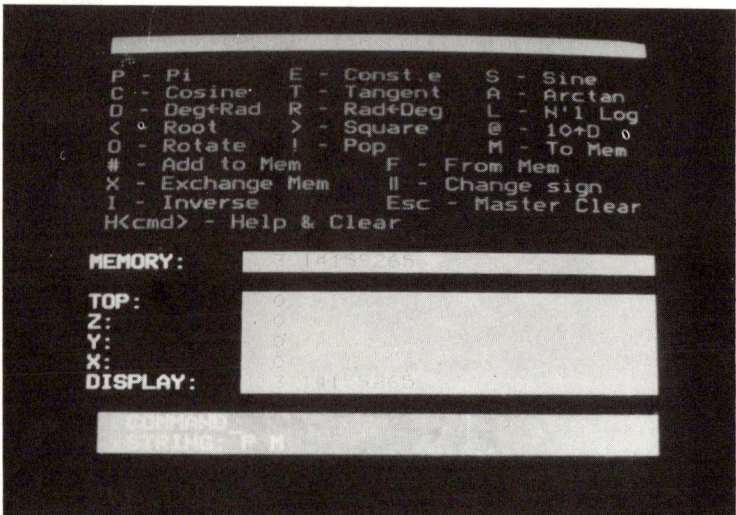

On typing RUN, the screen clears and immediately fills with the display shown in the illustration. The calculator is ready for use. PROCDISPLAY and PROCBOUNDS take care of this, and if we turn to the illustration, or the listing between lines 580 and 670, you will observe that a number of functions are offered at the touch of a key. You will know, or be able to guess at, most of the functions. Pressing the letter P, for example, immediately produces the value of pi ready for calculating with. However, there are some commands that may be strange, such as POP or ROTATE, and to understand these we need to look into RPN a little.

Using normal notation, we write 3 × 4, but in RPN we write 3, 4, × – the operator following the two numbers that it works upon – hence the 'reverse' of the title. To do this, we require a 'stack' upon which is stored the numbers to be worked on. The point about any stack (a stack of plates, for example) is that *last* item added to the stack is the *first* off; as distinct from a queue, in which the first in is the first out. In this computer program, we are using an upside-down stack capable of storing five items, which will be found to be more than enough for most purposes. I have called the five parts (a) Display – the item we see or work upon first, (b) X, (c) Y, (d) Z, and (e) Top. Follow the 3 × 4 example. We type 3 and press RETURN. 3 is entered into the Display register. Now we type 4 and press RETURN. The figure 4 appears in the Display register, but the 3 has moved up to the X register. Both are held separately. Typing * (for multiply) multiplies the bottom two registers together; 12 appears in the Display register, and the 3 and 4 disappear.

So what, you ask? Well, we have looked at a pathetically simple example. The real value of RPN comes when we start encountering brackets – the more the merrier. So as not to take too long over it, let's take another fairly simple example, 8 * ((4 − 2) + (5 − 1)). Working this conventionally, we find ourselves hopping backwards and forwards; we need to calculate 4 − 2 and store the result, then work 5 − 1, recover the sub-result (2) and add it to the other (4), making 6; then go back to the beginning to find the 8 and multiply, making 48.

In RPN, there is no hopping about. Type 8 (Return). Type 4 (Return). We cannot operate on those two yet, so we type the next, which is 2. We *can* operate on the 4 and 2, so we type '−' (no need for RETURN). Type 5 (Return). Type 1, −, +, *· The job is done! Note that we worked from left to right on the numbers, ignoring brackets, except to ask ourselves if we could operate on the last two numbers. Put succinctly, the entire command line, with (R) short for RETURN, is: 8 (R) 4 (R) 2 − 5 (R) 1 − + *·

There is really only one basic rule to remember; an operator such as + or * operates on the last two numbers on the stack – the bottom pair, in this program. An operator such as S (sine value) operates only on the bottom (Display) value.

Now I could spend a lot of time extolling the virtues of RPN and teaching the reader how to use it, but this is not a book on mathematics and I want to point out other features of this very useful and fascinating program.

In addition to the five-layer stack there is a Memory to which values can be assigned, added to, etc., but only from the Display register. Secondly, as you type commands – numbers or mnemonics – they appear in a growing 'Command String' at the bottom of the display, which is useful as a record of what you have done. Finally, there is a fully implemented HELP function. Pressing H at any time will bring you a succinct description of any of the displayed functions.

So to the POP and ROTATE. POP is a method of discarding the contents of the Display register; it is simply thrown away and the rest of the stack is dropped one position. Perhaps you can guess at ROTATE: the stack is rotated one place. That is, the Display value is moved to the TOP position, and all the rest dropped one place.

Finally, it's worth pointing out that apart from its value in teaching and utilising RPN, this program has value in teaching the user what a stack is and how it works. As the computer itself uses stacks, this should be of great interest to us. I can recommend a study of this program before you start thinking about using a language such as FORTH, for example.

Variables

S$	String of spaces for register clearance purposes
M	Value held in Memory
T	Value held in TOP register
X, Y, Z	Values in these registers
D	Value held in DISPLAY register
X$	Command string already executed
C$	Current command
A%	ASCII value of C$
Q	Temporary holding variable
K$	Start of line for blue on yellow
L$	Start of line for red text

```
10 ON ERROR GOTO 420
20 S$=STRING$(12," ")
30 Y$=CHR$131+CHR$157+CHR$132
40 B$=CHR$132+CHR$157+CHR$131
50 MODE7:M=0:T=0:Z=0:Y=0:X=0:D=0:X$="":PROCBOUNDS
60 PROCDISPLAY
70 REPEAT:PRINTTAB(0,20);B$;"YOUR COMMAND ";:INPUT C$:UNT
   IL C$<>""
80 IF X$="" X$=C$ ELSE X$=X$+" "+C$
90 PRINTTAB(0,21);B$;"STRING: ";X$
100 IF LEFT$(C$,1)="." C$="0"+C$
110 A%=ASC(LEFT$(C$,1))
120 IF A%>57 OR A%<48 GOTO140
130 C=VAL(C$):PROCUP:D=C:A%=ASC(RIGHT$(C$,1))
140 IF A%=33 D=X:PROCDOWN
150 IF A%=35 M=M+D
160 IF A%=42 D=D*X:PROCDOWN
170 IF A%=43 D=D+X:PROCDOWN
180 IF A%=45 D=X-D:PROCDOWN
190 IF A%=47 D=X/D:PROCDOWN
200 IF A%=60 D=SQR(D)
210 IF A%=62 D=D*D
220 IF A%=64 D=10↑D
230 IF A%=65 D=ATN(D)
240 IF A%=67 D=COS(D)
250 IF A%=68 D=DEG(D)
260 IF A%=69 PROCUP:D=2.71828183
270 IF A%=70 PROCUP:D=M
280 IF A%=72 PROCHELP:GOTO50
290 IF A%=73 D=1/D
300 IF A%=76 D=LOG(D)
310 IF A%=77 M=D
320 IF A%=79 Q=D:D=X:PROCDOWN:T=Q
330 IF A%=80 PROCUP:D=PI
340 IF A%=82 D=RAD(D)
350 IF A%=83 D=SIN(D)
360 IF A%=84 D=TAN(D)
370 IF A%=88 Q=M:M=D:D=Q
380 IF A%=94 D=X↑D:PROCDOWN
390 IF A%=124 D=-D
400 GOTO60
410
420 IF ERR=17 GOTO50
430 REPORT:PRINT"... PRESS RETURN":INPUT Q$:GOTO50
440
450 DEFPROCDISPLAY
460 PRINTTAB(0,12);"MEMORY:";TAB(10);Y$;M;S$'"TOP:";TAB(1
    0);Y$;T;S$'"Z:";TAB(10);Y$;Z;S$
470 PRINT"Y:";TAB(10);Y$;Y;S$'"X:";TAB(10);Y$;X;S$'"DISPLA
    Y:";TAB(10);Y$;D;S$
480 PRINTTAB(0,20),STRING$(39," ")
490 ENDPROC
500
510 DEFPROCBOUNDS
520 PRINTY$;"    REVERSE-POLISH CALCULATOR"'
```

```
    530 PRINTCHR$129;"P - Pi       E - Const.e  S - Sine"'CHR
$129;"C - Cosine   T - Tangent  A - Arctan"'CHR$129;"D - De
g<Rad   R - Rad<Deg   L - N'l Log"
    540 PRINTCHR$129;"< - Root     > - Square   @ - 10↑D"'CHR
$129;"O - Rotate   ! - Pop       M - To Mem"'CHR$129;"# - Ad
d to Mem     F - From Mem"'CHR$129;"X - Exchange Mem    ║ -
Change sign"
    550 PRINTCHR$129;"I - Inverse           Esc - Master Clear"'
CHR$129;"H<cmd> - Help & Clear"
    560 ENDPROC
    570
    580 DEFPROCUP
    590 T=Z:Z=Y:Y=X:X=D:ENDPROC
    600
    610 DEFPROCDOWN
    620 X=Y:Y=Z:Z=T:T=0:ENDPROC
    630
    640 DEFPROCHELP
    650 CLS:PRINT'':IF LEN(C$)>1 S%=ASC(RIGHT$(C$,1)):GOTO680
    660 PRINT"HELP PAGE"'"          "''
    670 INPUT "WHICH SYMBOL REQUIRES EXPLANATION",X$:S%=ASC(X$
):PRINT
    680 IF S%=33 PRINT"! = POP: The display value is discarded
and the stack dropped one position.":GOTO930
    690 IF S%=35 PRINT"# = ADD TO MEMORY: The display value is
added to the memory value.":GOTO930
    700 IF S%=42 PRINT"* = MULTIPLY: The display value is"'"re
placed by the product of X and D."'"D and X are lost and the
rest of the     stack is dropped.":GOTO930
    710 IF S%=43 PRINT"+ = ADD: The display value is"'"replace
d by the sum of X and D."'"D and X are lost and the rest of
the     stack is dropped.":GOTO930
    720 IF S%=45 PRINT"- = SUBTRACT: The display value is"'"re
placed by the result of subtracting  D from X."'"D and X ar
e lost and the rest of the     stack is dropped.":GOTO930
    730 IF S%=47 PRINT"/ = DIVIDE: The display value is"'"repl
aced by the result of dividing X by D and the rest of the st
ack is dropped.":GOTO930
    740 IF S%=60 PRINT"< = ROOT: The display value is"'"replac
ed by its square root.":GOTO930
    750 IF S%=62 PRINT"> = SQUARE: The display value is"'"repl
aced by its square.":GOTO930
    760 IF S%=64 PRINT"@ = 10↑D: The display value is"'"replac
ed by 10 to the power."'"Eg, 3 would be replaced by 1000.":G
OTO930
    770 IF S%=65 PRINT"A = ARCTAN: The display value is"'"repl
aced by its arctan value in"'"radians.  Used for finding an
angle"'"whose tangent is known.":GOTO930
    780 IF S%=67 PRINT"C = COSINE: The display value in"'"radi
ans is replaced by its cosine.":GOTO930
    790 IF S%=68 PRINT"D = RADIANS TO DEGREES: The radian"'"va
lue of the display is converted to    equivalent degrees.":G
OTO930
    800 IF S%<>69 GOTO820 ELSE PRINT"E = CONSTANT 'e': The sta
ck is moved"'"up and the constant 'e' (2.71828183)"'"is inse
rted at the bottom."'"TOP value is lost."''
```

```
    810 PRINT"NOTE: When included in a numeric"'"value, E is r
ead as scientific notation as in 3.4E6, which gives 3400000"
:GOTO930
    820 IF S%=70 PRINT"F = FROM MEMORY: The stack is moved up
 and the contents of memory are copied   into the display po
sition."'"TOP value is lost.":GOTO930
    830 IF S%=73 PRINT"I = INVERSE: The display value is"'"rep
laced by its inverse, ie, 1/D":GOTO930
    840 IF S%=76 PRINT"L = NATURAL LOGARITHM (BASE e): The"'"d
isplay value is replaced by its"'"natural logarithm.":GOTO93
0
    850 IF S%=77 PRINT"M = TO MEMORY: The display value is"'"c
opied into the memory.  Original"'"memory is lost.":GOTO930
    860 IF S%=79 PRINT"O = ROTATE STACK: The display value"'"i
s transferred to the top and the rest  of the stack is moved
down. Nothing is   lost.":GOTO930
    870 IF S%=80 PRINT"P = PI: The stack is moved up and the
 value Pi (3.14159265) is placed in the  display register."'
"TOP value is lost.":GOTO930
    880 IF S%=82 PRINT"R = DEGREES TO RADIANS: The display"'"v
alue is converted to radians.":GOTO930
    890 IF S%=83 PRINT"S = SINE: The radian display value is
 converted to sines.":GOTO930
    900 IF S%=84 PRINT"T = TANGENT: The radian display value
 is converted to tangent.":GOTO930
    910 IF S%=88 PRINT"X = EXCHANGE MEMORY: The display value
 and the memory are exchanged.":GOTO930
    920 IF S%=124 PRINT"¦ = CHANGE SIGN: Positive values in th
e display register are made negative and  vice-versa."
    930 INPUT''"Press RETURN....",A$:ENDPROC
```

27

Moses

This is a simulation in which you have to make decisions, the results of which interact with other conditions and events to produce other conditions. In short, one is conducting a sort of balancing act between conflicting necessities, learning the rules as one goes along. In that, it mirrors life, of course, which makes simulations so interesting.

As lines 20 and 30 of the listing say, the user has to help Moses guide the Israelites to the Promised Land. They have just crossed the Red Sea and in front of them is the Sinai Desert. As newly freed slaves they have no ability to survive in the desert, no fighting skills, no tribal or social cohesion, and no laws. The only thing that they

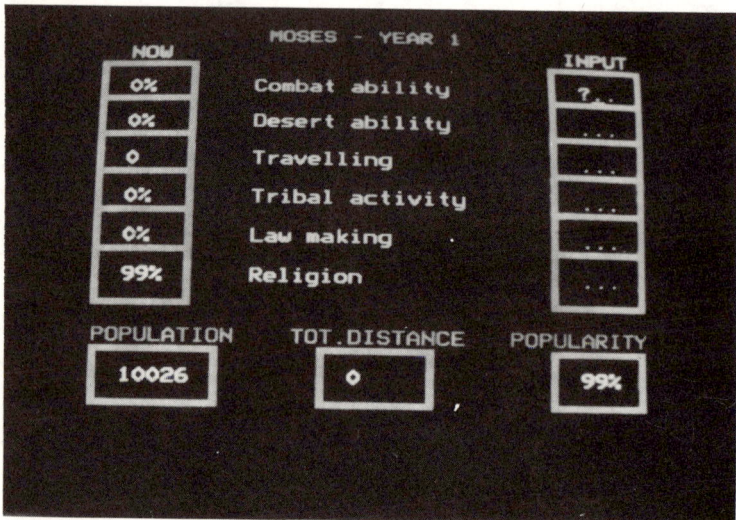

do have is a high standing in the sight of God, and the leadership of Moses — plus your help, of course! You win the game if, after 10 rounds or game years, you have travelled not less than 1000 miles to reach the River Jordan, achieved a popularity rating of not less than 80 per cent, retained standing with God of not less than 80 per cent, and achieved a combat ability of 80 per cent, too. The reasons (or excuses, if you like) are contained in lines 210 to 400 of the listing.

The listing is a long one, which may deter some people, but if you glance at the game loop, contained between lines 100 and 160, you will see that it is modular of course; what is more to the point, PROCEVENT can be omitted. In its turn, PROCEVENT calls no less than nine other procedures which would be omitted too. So if you don't like typing, or wish to sample the program before typing all of it in, omit line 140, and all lines 570 to 2270!

In play, on the left of the display is information about current conditions, and on the right are boxes for six inputs. The user is asked to divide up his time between these six, which entails decisions about the importance of each at every step. The six are: (a) combat ability, (b) desert survival skills, (c) travelling, (d) tribal or social activities, (e) law making, and (f) religious duties. Inputs take the form of percentages, with all adding up to 100 per cent. At the outset, how important is it that the Israelites should learn to fight and defend themselves, as against travelling or fulfilling their religious obligations? As we have said, these things interact: you will not travel far or fast if desert survival skills are low, while if your social cohesion is low, the population will fall off rapidly as old folk or the weak are left behind and the tribe begins to disintegrate. In the meantime, if you neglect religious duties, your standing in the eyes of God will fall off and He will support you less often in times

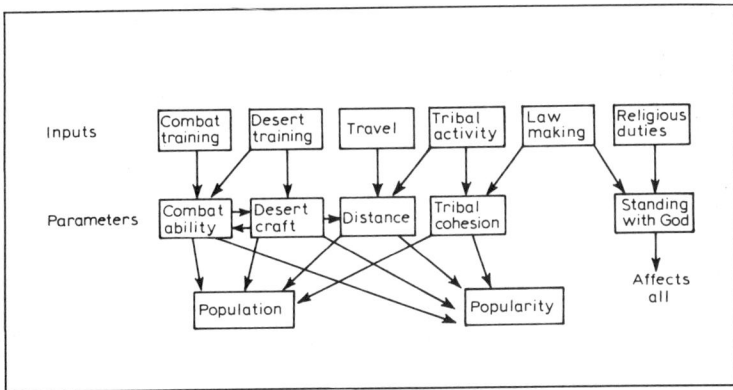

of need. The pattern of interaction is illustrated in the diagram. This is the model upon which the program was based and will bear close comparison with the mathematical model as carried out in PROC-CALCULATE beginning at line 2330.

When the user has made an input into the first five boxes, the program calculates the percentage remaining for the last and asks you if these inputs are all right. If so, the results are calculated. PROCEVENT is then called, which selects one of PROC-DROUGHT, PROCSTARVE, PROCFIGHT, PROCCOMMAND, PROCCALF, PROCFIRE, PROCPLAGUE, PROCMUTINY or PROC-QUAKE. These events too affect, and are affected by, existing conditions, with PROCLIMIT setting numeric limits on the parameters.

This cycle of input–event–output continues for nine game years and then performance is assessed.

Despite its length, the program is really rather simple, although a few of the procedures are interesting. PROCCOMMAND, for example, mixes up the Ten Commandments and asks the user to rearrange them. The variable F1 is a flag that prevents this procedure being used twice in one game. C%(X%) is an array with pointers to the Commandments; these pointers are mixed up and the appropriate DATA lines are read and printed in line 1330. This method of mixing the pointers rather than the texts themselves is not only much faster, but also effects an enormous saving of memory.

The user is required to type the number against the first Commandment, which is accepted in line 1370, is marked right or wrong, and then loops ten times. The score is given in line 1430. This procedure will stand on its own as a rather nice little program.

PROCCALF is another rather interesting procedure, requiring some thought on the part of the user, and could well be adapted for many types of program. The user is given a choice of six alternatives and asked to choose two of them. There is a call to PROCTWIN which accepts two single-digit inputs, putting them in variables G and H. Different combinations of digits are awarded different points in lines 1580 to 1630, the last three actually being penalised. The best pair is given a bonus in line 1640.

A similar arrangement takes place in PROCMUTINY (lines 1810 to 2010), with the additional provision that one particular digital response is considered to be fatal — see line 1930.

In line 2110 I have been rather naughty and many people will want to spank me for it. Strictly speaking, a procedure should be entirely self-contained, but as long as BASIC finds an ENDPROC command after a PROC, it doesn't care. What I *should* have done is to take lines 1720 to 1750 out of PROCFIRE and called it by another procedure name — perhaps PROCDEATHS. PROCFIRE and PROC-QUAKE would then each call PROCDEATHS. All three would of course end with an ENDPROC command. Don't do as I do — do as I say!

```
Put these in order -

1   Do not take the Lord's name in vain
2   Keep the Sabbath Day holy
3   Thou shalt not kill
4   Thou shalt not covet
5   Do not bear false witness
6   Do not make graven images
7   Do not commit adultery
8   Thou shalt not steal
9   Thou shalt have no other God
10  Honour thy father and mother

Position 1 - Number ?9   RIGHT!
Position 2 - Number ?_
```

Variables

A(13)   Game parameters, where:
         1 = Combat training input
         2 = Desert survival training input
         3 = Time spent travelling in current year
         4 = Time spent in social activities
         5 = Time given over to administration
         6 = Time given over to religious duties
         7 = Actual combat ability
         8 = Desert survival ability
         9 = Tribal cohesion
         10 = Standing with God
         11 = Population
         12 = Distance travelled in last game period
         13 = Popularity
X   General counter
F0   'Egyptians attack' flag
F1   '10 Commandments' flag
F2   'Golden Calf' flag
C%(10)   Commandments pointer array
T   Total distance travelled
SC%   Score
E%   Random event
L%   Population losses
N%   Commandment number
Y%   General counter
G,H   Digital inputs from PROCTWIN
G%   Losses to be mitigated by God
G$ General input string

```
 10 MODE7:PROCTITLE("MOSES")
 20 PRINT''"In which you lead the Children of"
 30 PRINT"Israel to the Promised Land.":PROCRET
 40 DIM A(13),C%(10)
 50 FORX=1TO13:A(X)=0:NEXT:F0=0:F1=0:F2=0
 60 A(10)=99:A(11)=9950+RND(100):A(13)=99:T=0
 70
 80 REM - Game loop
 90
100 FOR YEAR%=0 TO 9
110 PROCDISPLAY
120 PROCCALCULATE
130 IF RND(1)>.95 PROCNIL:GOTO150
```

```
140 PROCEVENT
150 PROCLIMIT
160 NEXT YEAR%
170
180 REM - Last year; assessment
190
200 CLS:IF T>=1000 GOTO240
210 PROCTITLE("TIME UP!")
220 PRINT''"You have not reached the River Jordan"
230 GOTO420
240 PROCTITLE("THE RIVER JORDAN!")
250 PRINT''CHR$131;"You have reached the River Jordan"''
260 IFA(13)>80 GOTO300
270 PRINT;"Your popularity is only ";A(13);"%"
280 PRINT"and the people will not follow you"
290 PRINT"across the river to the Promised Land.":GOTO420
300 IFA(10)>=80 GOTO340
310 PRINT;"Your standing with God is only ";A(10);"%"
320 PRINT"and He will not let you cross the river"
330 PRINT"into the Promised Land.":GOTO420
340 IFA(7)>=80 GOTO380
350 PRINT;"Your combat ability is only ";A(7);"%"
360 PRINT"and waiting on the other side of the river"
370 PRINT"are the enemy, much stronger than you.":GOTO420
380 PROCDBL(0,10,131,"YOU CROSS OVER INTO THE PROMISED LAND")
390 PROCDBL(5,13,133,CHR$136+"YOU WIN THE GAME!")
400 SC%=A(7)+A(8)+A(9)+2*A(10)+2*A(11)+A(13)
410 PRINT'';"YOUR SCORE IS ";SC%:END
420 PRINT''CHR$136;CHR$134;"SORRY - YOU LOSE":END
430
440 REM - Procedures start
450
460 DEFPROCLIMIT
470 FORX=7TO10:A(X)=INT(A(X))
480 IFA(X)>99 A(X)=99
490 IFA(X)<0A(X)=0
500 NEXT
510 IFA(13)>99A(13)=99
520 IFA(13)<0A(13)=0
530 A(11)=INT(A(11))
540 A(13)=INT(A(13))
550 ENDPROC
560
570 DEFPROCEVENT
580 IF T<100 AND RND(1)>.5 PROCEGYPT:ENDPROC
590 E%=RND(12)
600 ONE%GOTO630,610,620,630,640,650,660,670,680,690,630,630
610 PROCDROUGHT:ENDPROC
620 PROCSTARVE:ENDPROC
630 PROCFIGHT:ENDPROC
640 PROCCOMMAND:ENDPROC
650 PROCCALF:ENDPROC
660 PROCFIRE:ENDPROC
670 PROCPLAGUE:ENDPROC
680 PROCMUTINY:ENDPROC
```

```
690 PROCQUAKE:ENDPROC
700
710 DEFPROCDROUGHT
720 CLS:PROCTITLE("DROUGHT!")
730 IFA(10)>80 GOTO770
740 L%=(A(11)*(100-A(8))/100)*RND(1)
750 PROCGOD(L%)
760 A(11)=A(11)-L%:A(13)=A(13)-L%*.2:PROCRET
765 PRINT;''L%;" people die of thirst.":ENDPROC
770 PRINT'"God tells Moses where to strike the"
780 PRINT"desert with his rod. Water gushes out"
790 PRINT"and all can drink."
800 A(13)=A(13)+RND(10):PROCRET:ENDPROC
810
820 DEFPROCSTARVE
830 CLS:PROCTITLE("FAMINE!")
840 IFA(10)>80 GOTO890
850 L%=(A(11)*(100-A(8)))/100)*RND(1)
860 PROCGOD(L%)
870 PRINT;''L%;" people die of starvation."
880 A(11)=A(11)-L%:A(13)=A(13)-L%*.2:PROCRET:ENDPROC
890 PRINT'''"Moses shows the people how to find and"
900 PRINT"eat manna.":GOTO800
910
920 DEFPROCFIGHT
930 CLS:PROCTITLE("ATTACKED!"):RESTORE
940 FORA=1TORND(3):READQ$:NEXTA
950 PRINT''"You are attacked by the ";Q$
960 DATAAmelkites,Canaanites,Midianites
970 PROCLOSSES:ENDPROC
980
990 DEFPROCLOSSES
1000 L%=A(11)*(100-A(7))/100*RND(1):PROCGOD(L%)
1010 IF L%<25 GOTO1040
1020 PRINT''L%;" of your people are killed."
1030 A(11)=A(11)-L%:A(13)=A(13)-L%*.02:PROCRET:ENDPROC
1040 PRINT;'''"You win the battle, losing ";L%;" men."
1050 A(11)=A(11)-L%:A(13)=A(13)*1.125+20:PROCRET:ENDPROC
1060
1070 DEFPROCCOMMAND
1080 IF F1 ENDPROC
1090 DATAThou shalt have no other God
1100 DATADo not make graven images
1110 DATADo not take the Lord's name in vain
1120 DATAKeep the Sabbath Day holy
1130 DATAHonour thy father and mother
1140 DATAThou shalt not kill
1150 DATADo not commit adultery
1160 DATAThou shalt not steal
1170 DATADo not bear false witness
1180 DATAThou shalt not covet
1190 FORX%=1TO10:C%(X%)=0:NEXT
1200 REM - Mix them up
1210 FORX%=1TO10
1220 N%=RND(10):IFC%(N%)<>0GOTO1220
```

```
1230 C%(N%)=X%:NEXT X%
1240 CLS:PROCTITLE("THE TEN COMMANDMENTS")
1250 PRINT'"God handed down to Moses the Ten"
1260 PRINT"Commandments on tablets of stone.  Your"
1270 PRINT"job is to put them in order.":PROCRET
1280 CLS
1290 PROCDBL(2,1,131,CHR$131+CHR$136+"Put these in order -")
1300 PRINT
1310 FORX%=1TO10:PRINT;X%;" ";:RESTORE1090
1320 FORY%=1TOC%(X%):READX$*NEXT
1330 PRINTCHR$134;X$:NEXT:PRINT
1340 SC%=0
1350 FORX%=1TO10:REPEAT
1360 PRINT;CHR$131;"Position ";X%;" - Number ";
1370 INPUT Q%:UNTIL Q%>0 AND Q%<11:PRINTCHR$11;
1380 FORZ=1TO24:PRINTCHR$9;:NEXT
1390 IF C%(Q%)<>X% GOTO1410
1400 SC%=SC%+1:PRINTCHR$130;"RIGHT!":GOTO1420
1410 PRINTCHR$129;"WRONG"
1420 NEXT:A(10)=A(10)+3*SC%
1430 F1=1:PRINT"SCORE ";SC%;"/10":PROCRET:ENDPROC
1440
1450 DEFPROCCALF
1460 IF F2 ENDPROC
1470 CLS:PROCTITLE("THE GOLDEN CALF")
1480 PRINT'"Moses returns to camp to find that the"
1490 PRINT"people have made a golden calf and are"
1500 PRINT"worshipping it.";CHR$131;"What should he do - ?"
1510 PRINTCHR$130;"1 - Join them"
1520 PRINTCHR$130;"2 - Smash the calf"
1530 PRINTCHR$130;"3 - Do nothing"
1540 PRINTCHR$130;"4 - Think that they are stupid"
1550 PRINTCHR$130;"5 - Punish them"
1560 PRINTCHR$130;"6 - Have a special religious service"
1570 PROCTWIN
1580 IFG=2ORG=5 SC%=SC%+5
1590 IFG=6ORH=6 SC%=SC%+3
1600 IFH=2ORH=5 SC%=SC%+5
1610 IFH=1ORG=1 SC%=SC%-10
1620 IFG=3ORH=3 SC%=SC%-5
1630 IFG=4ORH=4 SC%=SC%-3
1640 IF(G=2ORG=5)AND(H=2ORH=5)SC%=SC%+5
1650 FORX%=1TO3:PRINTCHR$9;:NEXT
1660 PRINTCHR$131;"Score ";SC%;"/25":PROCRET
1670 A(10)=A(10)+SC%-10:A(13)=A(13)-SC%:F2=1:ENDPROC
1680
1690 DEFPROCFIRE
1700 CLS:PROCTITLE("FIRE IN CAMP!")
1710 PRINT''"There is a fire among your tents."
1720 L%=A(11)*(100-A(10))/100*RND(1):PROCGOD(L%)
1730 PRINT''L%;" people are killed."
1740 A(11)=A(11)-L%:A(13)=A(13)-L%*.2:PROCRET
1750 ENDPROC
1760
1770 DEFPROCPLAGUE
```

```
1780 CLS:PROCTITLE("PLAGUE!"):RESTORE
1790 PRINT''"Your people are struck by the plague.":GOTO1720
1800 DEFPROCMUTINY
1810 CLS:PROCTITLE("MUTINY!")
1820 PRINT'"The people shout,";CHR$129;"'Why did Moses bring"
1830 PRINTCHR$129;"us out of Egypt - to die in the desert?"
1840 PRINTCHR$129;"Down with Moses!'"
1850 PRINTCHR$135;"What should Moses do?"
1860 PRINTCHR$130;"1 - Leave them in the desert"
1870 PRINTCHR$130;"2 - Punch a few heads"
1880 PRINTCHR$130;"3 - Punish the ringleaders"
1890 PRINTCHR$130;"4 - Ask God to help him"
1900 PRINTCHR$130;"5 - Take them back to Egypt"
1910 PRINTCHR$130;"6 - Show them a few miracles."
1920 PROCTWIN
1930 IFG=1 OR H=1 PROCDONE
1940 IFG=2ORH=2SC%=SC%-5
1950 IFG=4ORH=4SC%=SC%+5
1960 IFG=6ORH=6SC%=SC%+5
1970 IF(G=6ORG=4)AND(H=6ORH=4)SC%=SC%+5
1980 IFG=3ORH=3SC%=SC%+3
1990 PRINTCHR$131;"SCORE ";SC%;"/25":SC%=SC%-10
2000 A(9)=A(9)+SC%*.5:A(10)=A(10)+SC%:A(13)=A(13)-SC%
2010 PROCRET:ENDPROC
2020
2030 DEFPROCDONE
2040 CLS:PROCTITLE("RESIGNATION")
2050 PRINT''"Since you do not want Moses to lead the"
2060 PRINT"people any longer, there is no point in continuing."
2070 PRINTCHR$130;"Goodbye!":END
2080
2090 DEFPROCQUAKE
2100 CLS:PROCTITLE("EARTHQUAKE!")
2110 PRINT''"Your camp is struck by an earthquake.":GOTO1720
2120
2130 DEFPROCEGYPT
2140 IF F0 THEN ENDPROC
2150 CLS:PROCTITLE("EGYPTIANS!"):RESTORE
2160 PRINT''"You are too near to Egypt. You are"
2170 PRINT"attacked by cavalry."
2180 PROCLOSSES:ENDPROC
2190
2200 DEFPROCGOD(G%)
2210 L%=G%*(100-A(10))/100*RND(1)*.5:IFL%<0 L%=0
2220 ENDPROC
2230
2240 DEFPROCNIL
2250 CLS:PROCTITLE("NOTHING TO REPORT")
2260 PRINT''"There have been no special events this  year."
2270 PROCRET:ENDPROC
2280
2290 DEFPROCRET
2300 PRINT''CHR$131;"Press";CHR$132;CHR$157;CHR$129;
2310 PRINT"RETURN ";CHR$156;:INPUTQ$:ENDPROC
2320
```

```
2330 DEFPROCCALCULATE
2340 REM - COMBAT ABILITY
2350 A(7)=A(1)*.7+A(2)*.1+A(4)*.07+A(5)*.1+A(7)*.825
2360 REM - DESERT SURVIVAL
2370 A(8)=A(2)*.72+A(3)*.1+A(7)*.05+A(8)*.77+A(9)*.1
2380 REM - TRIBAL COHESION
2390 A(9)=A(9)*.8+A(1)*.1-A(3)*.1+A(4)*.7+A(5)*.8
2400 A(9)=A(9)+A(6)*.1+A(8)*.1
2410 REM - STANDING WITH GOD
2420 A(10)=A(5)*.2+A(6)*.6+A(10)*.8
2430 REM - POPULATION
2440 P=A(11)
2450 A(11)=A(11)*.99-(A(1)+A(2)+A(3))*.2+A(4)*.65
2460 A(11)=A(11)+A(5)*.55+A(8)*.87+A(9)*.3
2470 REM - DISTANCE COVERED
2480 A(12)=INT(A(3)*.21*(A(8)*.175+A(9)*.1)-A(11)*.005)
2490 IFA(12)<5 A(12)=INT(A(3)*.1)
2500 T=T+A(12)
2510 REM - POPULARITY
2520 A(13)=A(13)*.925-(A(1)+A(2)+A(3))*.1+A(5)*.25
2530 A(13)=A(13)+A(6)*.3+A(8)*.2-(100-A(9))*.3
2540 A(13)=A(13)-(P-A(11))*.025+A(4)*.66
2550 ENDPROC
2560
2570 DEFPROCbox(L%,H%,C%)
2580 LOCALV%,W%,I%,J%
2590 V%=VPOS:W%=POS
2600 PRINTTAB(W%,V%-H%);CHR$(C%+144);"7";
2610 FORI%=0TOL%+1:PRINT"£";:NEXT:PRINT"k"
2620 PRINTTAB(W%,V%+1);CHR$(C%+144);"u";
2630 FORI%=0TOL%+1:PRINT"p";:NEXT:PRINT"z"
2640 FORJ%=V%-H%+1TOV%:PRINTTAB(W%,J%);CHR$(C%+144);"5";CHR$135
2650 NEXT
2660 FORJ%=V%-H%+1TOV%
2670 PRINTTAB(W%+L%+3,J%);CHR$(C%+144);"j":NEXT
2680 PRINTTAB(W%+3,V%);"";
2690 IF NOT(FLAG) ENDPROC
2700 FORI%=1TOL%:PRINT".";:NEXT
2710 PRINTTAB(W%+3,V%);
2720 ENDPROC
2730
2740 DEFPROCDISPLAY
2750 X$=CHR$133+"MOSES - YEAR "+STR$(YEAR%+1)+""
2760 DATACombat ability,Desert ability,Travelling
2770 DATATribal activity,Law making,Religion
2780 CLS:PRINTTAB(12);X$'"  NOW";TAB(34);"INPUT"
2790 RESTORE 2760:FOR X=3TO13STEP 2:READ X$
2800 PRINTTAB(11,X);CHR$131;;X$;:PRINTTAB(0,X);
2810 FLAG=FALSE:PROCbox(3,1,4):PRINTTAB(32,X);
2820 FLAG=TRUE:PROCbox(3,1,4):NEXT
2830 PRINTTAB(0,16);CHR$130;
2840 PRINT"POPULATION   TOT.DISTANCE   POPULARITY"
2850 PRINTTAB(0,18);:FLAG=FALSE:PROCbox(5,1,4)
2860 PRINTTAB(16,18);:PROCbox(4,1,4)
2870 PRINTTAB(32,18);:PROCbox(3,1,4)
```

```
2880 PRINTTAB(3,3);A(7);"%";
2890 PRINTTAB(3,5);A(8);"%";
2900 PRINTTAB(3,7);A(12);
2910 PRINTTAB(3,9);A(9);"%";
2920 PRINTTAB(3,11);A(5);"%";
2930 PRINTTAB(3,13);A(10);"%";
2940 PRINTTAB(3,18);A(11);
2950 PRINTTAB(19,18);T;
2960 PRINTTAB(35,18);A(13);"%";
2970 I%=100:FOR X%=1TO5:PRINTTAB(35,X%*2+1);
2980 INPUTX:IF X>I% PROCtoobig:GOTO2750
2990 A(X%)=X:I%=I%-X:NEXT:A(6)=I%
300C PRINTTAB(35,13);I%;"%";
3010 PRINTTAB(0,21);"Are those figures OK (Y-N)?";
3020 REPEAT:G$=GET$:UNTILG$="Y"ORG$="N":IF G$="N"GOTO2750
3030 ENDPROC
3040
3050 DEFPROCDBL(X%,Y%,C%,X$)
3060 PRINTTAB(X%,Y%);CHR$141;CHR$C%;X$
3070 PRINTTAB(X%,Y%+1);CHR$141;CHR$C%;X$:ENDPROC
3080
3090 DEFPROCTITLE(X$)
3100 PRINTCHR$132;STRING$(19,"Oo")
3110 PROCDBL((36-LEN(X$))/2,4,131,X$)
3120 PRINTCHR$132;STRING$(19,"Oo")
3130 ENDPROC
3140
3150 DEFPROCinput:X$=""
3160 G$=GET$:IF ASCG$=13 GOTO3230
3170 IF ASCG$<>127GOTO3200
3180 IF X$="" GOTO 3160 ELSE X$=LEFT$(X$,1)
3190 GOTO3160
3200 IF ASCG$<=47 OR ASCG$>=58 GOTO3160
3210 PRINT;G$;:X$=X$+G$
3220 IFLENX$<>2 GOTO 3160 ELSE 3240
3230 IFX$=""PRINT;" 0";
3240 IFLENX$=1PRINTCHR$8;" ";VALX$;
3250 PRINT;"%":X=VALX$:ENDPROC
3260
3270 DEFPROCtoobig
3280 PRINTTAB(0,22);"The total of all six input boxes cannot"
3290 PRINT"be greater than 100%.  Press RETURN and"
3300 PRINT"try again...";:INPUTQ$:ENDPROC
3310 DEFPROCTWIN
3315
3320 PRINT''"TYPE";CHR$136;"TWO";CHR$137;"CHOICES ";
3330 PROCbox(2,1,4):REPEAT:G=GET:UNTIL G-48>=1 AND G-48<=6
3340 PRINTCHR$G;
3350 REPEAT:H=GET:UNTIL H-48>=1 AND H-48<=6 AND G<>H
3360 PRINTCHR$H;
3370 G=G-48:H=H-48:SC%=10
3380 ENDPROC
```